THE
CURIOUS LEADER

Unlocking *Innovation*,
Empowering *Teams*,
and Driving *Change*

JON BASSFORD, JD, MBA, CAE

The Curious Leader © Copyright 2025 Jonathan Bassford

All rights reserved. No part of this publication may be reproduced, distributed, or transmitted in any form or by any means, including photocopying, recording, or other electronic or mechanical methods, without the prior written permission of the publisher, except in the case of brief quotations embodied in critical reviews and certain other noncommercial uses permitted by copyright law.

Although the author and publisher have made every effort to ensure that the information in this book was correct at press time, the author and publisher do not assume and hereby disclaim any liability to any party for any loss, damage, or disruption caused by errors or omissions, whether such errors or omissions result from negligence, accident, or any other cause.

The advice and strategies found within may not be suitable for every situation. This work is sold with the understanding that neither the author nor the publisher is held responsible for the results accrued from the advice in this book.

All stories and lessons shared in this book are based on real events and experiences. However, for privacy and storytelling purposes, some details, such as locations, genders, and products, have been altered.

For more information, email jon@jonbassford.com.

ISBN PAPERBACK: 978-1-962280-78-5

ISBN EBOOK: ISBN: 978-1-962280-79-2

Reflek Publishing.

Dedicated to my wife, son, mother, and all those who supported my personal and professional journey.

TABLE OF CONTENTS

Introduction i
    Why Curiosity Is Necessary for Growth and Change .. viii
    Inevitability of Change xi

Chapter 1: Characteristics and Shifts Required in Becoming a Curious Leader 1
    Learning: The Foundation for Continuous Growth 2
    Adaptability: Thriving in the Face of Uncertainty 5
    Asking the Right Questions: The Catalyst
    for Innovation 7
    Seeking Diverse Perspectives: The Power
    of Collective Insight 9
    Seeing Problems from Different Perspectives:
    Unlocking Creative Solutions 11
    "Why Aren't We Amazon?" 13
    Three Shifts Required for Curiosity, Growth,
    and Innovation 15
        From a Fixed Mindset to a Growth Mindset 15
        Operational Excellence 16
        Fostering a Curious Culture 18

Chapter 2: Shifting from a Fixed Mindset to a Growth Mindset in Becoming a Curious Leader 21
    Understanding Fixed vs Growth Mindset 21
    Why Leaders Need a Growth Mindset 22
    Learning and Development Fuel Leadership Growth ... 26
    Adaptability Is Crucial in a Rapidly
    Changing World 28
    Belief in Oneself 29

The Shift: Moving from Fixed to Growth Mindset 33
   Acknowledge Your Fixed Mindset Tendencies 33
   Reframe Failure as Learning 34
   Seek Feedback and Be Open to Critique 35
   Celebrate Effort and Progress, Not Just Results 36
   Becoming a Curious Leader Through a Growth Mindset ... 36

Jeff Bezos, The Rise of Amazon and Beyond 37
   Amazon's Growth Through Bezos's Growth Mindset 38
   Other Ventures Fueled by Growth-Oriented Thinking 38
   Impact of Bezos's Growth Mindset on His Legacy 39

The Dangers of a Fixed Mindset 39

Chapter 3: Servant Leadership and Curiosity 45

Understanding the Principles of Servant Leadership 47

Curiosity Enhances Servant Leadership 49

Building Relationships Through Genuine
Interest in Others 51

Empowering and Uplifting Staff Through
Curious Engagement 53

The Resurgence of Microsoft Through
CEO Nadella 54
   Focusing on Collaboration and Empowerment 55
   Innovating with Empathy and Customer-Centricity 55
   Driving Cultural Change for Sustainable Growth 55

Chapter 4: Become Curious About Your Staff
to Maximize Potential 57

The Value of Understanding Individual
Strengths and Weaknesses 58

Reverse the View on the Younger Generation 60

Techniques for Gathering Insights About Staff 62

Personalized Development Plans 65

Fostering a Sense of Belonging and Motivation 66

Chapter 5: Building a Culture of Curiosity 69

Creating an Environment That Encourages
Questions and Curiosity.. 72

Allowing and Valuing Input and Feedback
from Staff.. 75

Starting with the New Person: Fresh Eyes in
Building a Curious Culture.. 79

Building Curiosity Through New
Employee Feedback.. 81

Beyond the New Hire: Creating a Curious
Culture for Everyone 83

Overcoming Non-Curious Environments 86

The Long-Term Payoff 87

Integrating Curiosity Into Organizational
Values and Practices... 89

Measuring and Celebrating Curiosity-
Driven Successes 90

Curiosity Tips: Use Improv in Brainstorming Sessions..91
 The Rules of Improv and Why They Work................... 92
 How Improv Leads to Innovation, Growth, and Change... 93

The Foundation of Psychological Safety....................... 94
 *The Aristotle Project: What It Was and
   Why It Mattered* 95
 The Key Finding: Psychological Safety 96
 Building Psychological Safety for a Curious Culture......... 97

Chapter 6: Evaluating Operations for Excellence 99

The Importance of Asking the Right
Questions and Driving Change 100

Tools and Techniques for Effective Questioning 105
Seeking External Help 107
Analyzing and Improving Business Processes 108
Systems and Methodologies for
    Process Improvement 114
Case Study: The Micromanaging Manager 115
Four Operational Areas to Assess for
    Excellence in Your Organization 116
    Decision-Making Framework 117
    Adaptability (People's Capacity for Change) and Culture 120
    Operational Strength 123
    Operational Efficiency 125
Interconnected Foundations of
    Operational Excellence 127

Chapter 7: Desired Business Outcomes of Curiosity-Driven Leadership 129

Defining Success Through the Lens of Curiosity 130
Enhanced Innovation and Problem-
    Solving Capabilities 133
NASA Leaders Breaking from Norms
    in *The Martian* 136
Increased Employee Engagement and Retention 138
Improved Decision-Making and Strategic Planning 141
Measurable Business Growth and Sustainability 142

Chapter 8: Overcoming Barriers to Curiosity 145

Identifying and Addressing Fears
    Related to Curiosity 146
    Four Types of Fears and Ways to Overcome Them 146
Innovation Policies 149

Recognizing the Impact of Ego on Curiosity 151
    Cultivating Humility and Openness to New Ideas.......... 151
    Strategies for Reducing Ego-Driven Resistance............. 152

Resistance.. 153
    Tactics for Overcoming Organizational Inertia 153
    When You Are the Problem 155
    Leveraging Change Management Principles to
       Foster Curiosity 157

Chapter 9: Immediate Actionable Steps for Leading with Curiosity 161

Clear Your Mind for Innovation 161

Questioning Everything: Leaving No
    Stone Unturned 163

Fresh Perspectives and Diverse Inputs 165

Gathering Data: Present and Future........................... 168

Impact and Outcomes 170

Setting a Strategic Path 172

Embracing Failure: Learning from Mistakes 175
    Key Elements of Innocent's Strategic Path 176
    Impact of Innocent's Strategic Path 178

Curiosity in Action: Sustaining the Momentum 181

Conclusion: Curiosity in Action—Driving Innovation, Growth, and Change 183

The Growth Mindset Shift: Transforming
    How You and Your Team Learn 184

Operations Excellence: Building Curiosity
    Into Processes 184

Creating a Curious Culture: Fostering an

    Environment Where Curiosity Thrives 184
    Call to Action for Leaders to Embrace Curiosity 185
    Leadership and Curiosity Are a Process 185
    Future Outlook on Curiosity and Leadership 187

Acknowledgments 189

About the Author 191

Endnotes 193

INTRODUCTION

"No man ever steps in the same river twice, for it's not the same river and he's not the same man."
—Heraclitus, *Fragments*

The speed with which the world is changing presents challenges, and a leader's effectiveness is more critical today than ever. The quote by Heraclitus overshadows an important fact of life: things are always changing. Those who are willing to change with the world around them and have the foresight and confidence to lead the change are ahead of the curve. Inevitably, change brings challenges. However, with every challenge, there is the opportunity to innovate, grow, and change to grow as individuals and drive results for the organizations we run.

Along with the classic leadership traits of decisiveness, confidence, and vision, another quality is becoming increasingly important: curiosity. By curiosity, I don't mean just a fundamental love of information. I'm talking about a desire to discover, explore, question, and understand the challenges that define our surroundings. It's about being creative in finding new and exciting ways to operate and solve our problems—to innovate, grow, and change.

I have to admit that curiosity as a leadership quality was not immediately apparent to me as I was building my professional career and working to build my leadership skills. However, there was a time when I was pursuing a change in my career and did what most people do. I dusted off the old digital rolodex (also known as LinkedIn). A friend from college asked if she could introduce me to her colleague who helps individuals discover their superpowers. Of course, I was willing and *curious*. After all, I consider myself self-aware and enjoy taking personality assessments to see how things match up.

This was not just your typical psychometric questionnaire. Instead, it involved working with an academic expert. After some discussions and forms, he revealed my superpower to be curiosity. Although I saw the importance of the power, it did not overly resonate with me. I was known for many attributes as my career progressed, and this was a new concept. Couldn't I get something cool like flight or invisibility?

Fast-forward ten or so years. I was doing work with a branding company that included a deep dive into me, my business, and the value we bring. Once again, the notion that curiosity as my superpower came up.

The fact that two strangers brought this up years apart demanded my attention, and my *curiosity* drove me to analyze my life and my career. The analysis helped me see just how much curiosity had driven my personal life as well as my career—including my curiosity and courage to explore, question, and seek out opportunities when I was a kid. This brought about amazing experiences and helped shape my worldview and create lasting values and desires for my life. One quick note on this exploration is seen in me now living in the DC Metro area that became a goal of mine after visiting DC on a family vacation in high school and then reaffirmed when I spent a semester in DC through the Washington Semester Program at American University.

Curiosity also became immediately evident when I examined my career. Curiosity had always been there. I am known for bringing an analytical, fresh eye to evaluating people, processes, and systems in the effort to drive efficiency and results in an organization. That was also showcased in my inherent ability to utilize resources at my disposal to analyze problems and find solutions. These combined skills allowed me to make a lasting impact on organizations I worked with and elevated my career. The analytical and problem-solving skillsets combined with my diverse knowledge and understanding led to a great career helping organizations grow through operations.

I could recognize my curiosity at work, even in the first month of my first professional job. Unsure about what I wanted to do after law school, I was curious and eager to explore a variety of options. I ended up falling into a position with an organization I'd been a member of in law school. A huge bonus: The job relocated me to Baltimore, which was just down the road from my goal city—Washington, DC. I took a job that was never on my radar that got me headed the direction I wanted to go physically and became the springboard for my entire career and leadership growth.

Coming off an amazing training trip with a colleague, I was puzzled by a very important piece of information. I was being told what our regional/chapter leaders were supposed to be doing, but I could not find it in writing anywhere. I was looking for that physical piece of evidence that I could point people to (albeit virtually).

These leaders and their activities were literally the lifeblood of our organization. They were the primary source of revenue and the majority of programming. I was being told about the basic minimum details about certain activities our leaders should be conducting and when. But, again, where was this documented? Where was this written down? Where was something tangible I could show the leaders?

Upon my return, I walked into my supervisor's office and asked a very simple question: "Where is this information?" I reminded him that I was being told these facts but didn't know where they existed. I wanted to put something in front of these people I was supposed to be training. Where was the manual, the bylaws, the website . . . *anything* that explained that these were the activities each and every leader, at a minimum, was expected to perform?

He had the answer to my very simple question: the back of a training manual. Training sessions generally happened for our leaders every fall, but they were held at different times because they were handled by each district and were in person. So, I had a few more questions that got answers.

I asked, "What if I don't go to a district conference? Will I ever see this?"

"Most likely not," my supervisor said.

"If I leave my manual at a conference, will I ever see it again?"

"Probably not."

"So, there is a good chance that someone receives these instructions in writing just *one* time in their entire tenure?"

"Yes, that is very possible."

And then my most impactful question: "Can I change that?"

And the answer was yes.

I did not make a sweeping vision or mission change to impact the organization. My curiosity just demanded to know how these leaders could more readily know what their duty was. So, I took this document out of the back of the manual, created a two-sided PDF, and used it with every instruction I gave to the leaders for the next six years.

When they asked about their calendars, I referenced the document. When asked about recruitment, I referenced the document.

That PDF became the lifeblood of how I ran my department and drove innovation, growth, and change. Due to its success, other departments followed suit.

So, what were our results?

- 20 percent increase in members and revenue
- 500 percent increase in programming
- Record-breaking attendance at events

This was not a negligent organization or staff. In fact, in the decade before I arrived, it experienced tremendous growth and had transitioned from a volunteer-run to a staff-run organization. This is important to point out because it is far easier to improve an organization that is doing nothing right. But that was not the case here. Most organizations are not overtly negligent. But, over time, they tend to settle into familiar habits and routines, which can unintentionally stifle fresh perspectives and limit critical analysis. The organizational leader had led the way but as things settled in, there was a small piece that was missed. My ability to bring a fresh eye, objectivity, and curiosity allowed me to take the great changes leaders before me made and take them to an even higher level.

When leaders think of growth and change, they envision these big, sweeping changes—restructuring, introducing new products, and more. But this is an excellent example of how simple curiosity ("Where is this located?") and small questions can drive tremendous change and growth! Curiosity and the right questions keep operations fresh because they encourage people to constantly see how things can be improved.

Curiosity in modern-day business is very much needed. We are no longer working on manufacturing lines and being asked to assemble the exact same part a hundred times a day. Our organizations are integrated, collaborative, fast-moving, and always changing. Curiosity is the key to ensuring that we continue to grow through that.

Curious leaders can cope better with the ever-changing nature of today. They also influence others in their environment by adapting to these changes and moving themselves and their teams to success. The flexibility and resilience fostered by high levels of curiosity can aid leaders in anticipating trends, being agile in responding to new needs, and changing strategies to stay ahead of the game. Curiosity is about constantly analyzing what we are doing and why we are doing it so we can make the path before us the most efficient and effective way to drive the results we seek.

Curiosity is not needed for every leader: Leaders wanting to stay in the status quo need not apply. Through my consulting work, I interact with organizational leaders daily who say, "We have been running this business for ten years, and we are doing just fine." Now, given my interaction with one such business leader, I was already aware that they were late on paying employment taxes, had no understanding of their finances, and were operating by the seat of their pants. However, curiosity is a must for leaders who stay ahead of the curve, improve their operations, innovate, grow, and change. It is far less important for those not interested in growth, sustainability, excellence, and time freedom.

> **Leadership isn't a destination—it's a journey.**

Before we embark on this journey together, let me take a moment to guide you on how best to approach this book. *The Curious Leader* is not just a road map—it's a conversation. It's built on stories, strategies, and insights gathered from years of successes and, equally importantly, failures. These pages are designed to spark reflection, provoke questions, and inspire action and not just inform. The goal is to inspire others to adopt more curiosity in their leadership to innovate, grow, and change.

Each chapter is structured to help you explore a specific aspect of curiosity-driven leadership, from cultivating a growth mindset to creating a culture where innovation thrives. Some chapters may resonate with your current challenges, while others might feel more aspirational, offering guidance for future stages of your leadership journey.

I encourage you to read with an open mind and a willingness to reflect on your experiences. Highlight sections that speak to you. Write notes in the margins. Pause at the end of each chapter to ask yourself, *How does this apply to me? To my team? To my organization?*

One of the lessons I've learned through my own leadership journey is that progress doesn't come from finding a one-size-fits-all solution. It comes from experimentation, from trying new ideas to see what fits. It comes from picking up nuggets of information, suggestions, and strategies that you can use along your journey. Use this book as a tool kit, picking up the pieces that work best for you and your team.

Leadership isn't a destination—it's a journey. And curiosity is the fuel that keeps that journey alive. So, as you read, I challenge you to step into this process fully: Question the status quo, embrace the discomfort of change, and celebrate the moments of growth along the way. Together, let's explore what it means to lead with curiosity and build something extraordinary.

WHY CURIOSITY IS NECESSARY FOR GROWTH AND CHANGE

Humans are creatures of habit and safety. And being curious is not always the easiest mode to slip into. Our evolutionary brains are programmed to keep us where we are. It's the old fight-or-flight mentality of human nature. These instincts exist to do one thing—keep us safe.

Habits serve many valuable functions in our daily lives, providing us with a sense of stability and efficiency. A deep dive into habits shows that we would be paralyzed by thought in everyday actions without habits. However, when it comes to innovation, growth, and change, habits are a direct and significant hindrance. This reality holds true whether you are striving to grow as an individual, leading an organization, or running a business. Since we run our organizations, our habits become their habits. Habits, routines, and one-track minds create barriers to innovation, change, and growth. Furthermore, the desire to play it safe and limit dreams and visions results in additional hurdles.

For a curious leader, recognizing the limitations imposed by habits and fears is the first step in fostering a culture of curiosity and continuous improvement. To break free from these limitations, it's crucial to step back and evaluate our situations objectively. Stagnation occurs when we become so entrenched in our routines that we continue to repeat actions, expecting different results—which is the definition of insanity. Science has shown that by the time we are about thirty-five, 90 percent of our actions and decisions are completely habitual. We even repeat the same actions for five, ten, or thirty years because it works. Then we're surprised when the change around us finally catches up and we find ourselves flatfooted. Famous psychologist Abraham Maslow said, "In any given moment, we have two options: to step forward into growth or to step back into safety."[1] Becoming a curious leader is all about stepping into growth.

Habits, routines, and one-track minds create barriers to innovation, change, and growth.

Although we typically think of habits in terms of actions, the same paralysis to growth can afflict our mindsets and the organizations we lead. Consider the founder who rigidly clings to their original vision for the organization despite shifts in technology, industry trends, and competitive landscapes. Or the founder who knows things are not right with operations but is just too afraid to step outside their comfort zone. In working with many organizational leaders, entrepreneurs, and business owners, I've found that these hindrances are all too common. The result is that, at the least, they stay exactly where they are. But more than likely, they will start to regress due to their inability to adapt to the world that's changing around them.

When thinking of the ever-changing world and our business landscapes, I find it an important time to raise Heraclitus's famous quote again, "No man ever steps in the same river twice, for it's not the same river and he's not the same man."[2] Change is inevitable. You either change with the flowing river or get left behind. Too many leaders and organizations fail to put in the proper measures, checks, and balances to ensure that they are continually adapting to change and daring to challenge what they are doing. Because habits and programming are natural, you have to create systems to break from them.

To break these cycles, we need to nurture curiosity within ourselves and our organizations. Curiosity encourages us to question the status quo, explore new possibilities, and adapt to changing circumstances. By doing so, we cultivate environments that are ripe for innovation, growth, and change. This is not change for the sake of changing. It's the driving force behind reaching new heights and tackling new problems. The future belongs to those who dare to ask, learn, and evolve continuously.

INEVITABILITY OF CHANGE

When you commit to being a curious leader, change becomes inevitable. You are no longer just responding to the change around you but actively working to improve, tweak, and adapt staying ahead of external changes. I've been hired many times to bring a fresh perspective, ask the hard questions, and drive improvement. But I've learned that change isn't always easy, nor is it always warmly received. I've worked on projects where my recommendations led to restructuring, and in some cases, that meant people had to leave. These moments are tough, and I've seen how change can create resentment or discomfort among team members. There was one particular instance when I pushed for a new approach that would **streamline operations and improve efficiency, yet a few longtime team members felt it was an overstep**—a disruption to the comfortable processes they were used to.

In moments like these, I've done my best to lead with empathy and clear communication, knowing that change, while necessary, requires care. A culture consultant I once worked with put it bluntly: "If people aren't leaving or you're not letting people go, you're not creating enough change." This doesn't mean change should be reckless. But it's a reminder that **significant transformations often demand difficult decisions and may disrupt the status quo**. And that's okay. That's kind of the point. And not everyone will be along for that ride.

In times of real stress and difficulty, we may need to make these sweeping changes to keep the organization adaptable and competitive. Not everyone will embrace change, and some may resist it outright. However, once curiosity is **embedded as part of your organization, you'll find it easier to** bring on board people who align with this adaptive mindset from the beginning. As my good friend and colleague Steven

Mandurano often says, "Change is hard in the beginning, messy in the middle, and amazing at the end." And that's the essence of curiosity-driven leadership: embracing the journey, welcoming the challenge, and trusting that, despite the messiness along the way, the results will be worth it in the end.

To be fair, the quote above is actually closely related to one by author Robin Sharma[3], but since Steven is the one who introduced it to me, he deserved some credit too.

CHAPTER 1
CHARACTERISTICS AND SHIFTS REQUIRED IN BECOMING A CURIOUS LEADER

"Be curious, not judgmental."
—Ted Lasso

Curiosity is often thought of as the birthright of the inventor, the scientist, and the researcher. But curiosity is the lifeblood of leadership itself: the heartbeat of growth, adaptability, and long-term sustainability. If you're trying to be a curious leader, it will take time to learn and experience how to bring more curiosity into your context. Although some individuals tap into curiosity more naturally, the great thing is that any leader can take steps to foster curiosity in themselves and their organizations. As mentioned above, it's about creating the mechanisms and systems to break from habits and programming. They can become a curious leader when it comes to creating contexts where curiosity shows up, is invited in, and is baked into every decision or action in the organization. Developing specific characteristics and making some fundamental shifts are crucial to becoming that curious leader.

LEARNING: THE FOUNDATION FOR CONTINUOUS GROWTH

At the heart of curious leadership is a commitment to continual learning. Curious leaders learn wherever they go; they learn from their environment, from their teams, and even from their competitors. They are lifelong learners. They see learning as a constantly moving target, an almost endless pursuit that allows them to stay on the cutting edge of trends, spot new opportunities, and lead teams using the latest insights and management techniques. Learning isn't just learning to grow one's personal development and knowledge but learning and analyzing how we are operating.

When I am faced with a challenge for a client or even my own organization, the first thing I do is look at my competition. What are they doing? What is their offer? How are they positioning themselves? What are their leaders putting out on social media? There is plenty of information and intel all around us. We just need a little curiosity about what to look for.

There are many great examples among modern-day and historic leaders who exemplify the concepts of continuous learning. It would actually be difficult to find someone known for leadership and innovation who is *not* known for their hunger for continual learning.

Benjamin Franklin, one of the Founding Fathers of the United States, is an exemplar of lifelong learning. Franklin (1706–1790) was a Renaissance man who epitomized the dedicated pursuit of knowledge in diverse fields. He was, among many other things, a statesman, inventor, writer, philosopher, and scientist. His traits of self-improvement and lifelong learning helped shape his many accomplishments.

Franklin's self-education throughout his life was a major source of the scientific and technological inventions that won him fame. He made his most well-known discovery when he concluded through his 1752 empirical kite experiment that lightning is electricity, which made him a celebrity abroad. But electricity was just one in a score of fields in which he applied his inquiring mind.

Benjamin Franklin provides a potent example of the power of lifelong learning to influence the lives and legacies of leaders. The span of his intellectual interests—from self-educated printer to scientific genius, from early businessman to wise statesman, and from electrical engineer to sage who touched countless lives—inspired others to reason and think rationally. At the same time, he showed remarkable kindness and generosity of spirit along the way.

For leaders, Franklin's life is a reminder that:

- Education does not end at school. Leaders need to keep learning—acquiring knowledge, new skills, and experience—to stay relevant and ahead of the curve. Throughout my career, I have dived headfirst into every role and organization so I could consume as much information as possible.
- Self-improvement is a long and winding road. Ben Franklin's systematic approach illustrates that learning is as much a process of self-cultivation as acquisition. I continually invest in myself through coaching and masterminds.
- Innovation frequently springs from diffuse curiosity and practical education. Franklin's immense slate of scientific inventions and civic accomplishments directly resulted from his sustained commitment to curiosity

and learning. I do not excel once my roles become stagnant. I want my career and the organizations I help to keep growing and moving forward.

The example Benjamin Franklin set for us all in his own learning journey demonstrates the interrelatedness of digestive powers and creative personal passion for human progress.

As an operations professional, you have to know a little about *everything*. There is no formal education that prepares you for a career in operations. At most, you may be lucky to have a formal education on one or two elements and learn the rest on the job. Throughout my career, I have had to learn new software, understand new business philosophies, and realize how culture affects results. I've even had the privilege of diving in headfirst to learn how to expand operations (logistically) to another continent. The ability to keep learning has been an element of my curiosity that has elevated my career.

One reason an operations professional may lack education is that the position can mean different things in different industries. For most small businesses, nonprofits, and even many Fortune 500 companies, the head of operations oversees internal functions and, often, day-to-day operations. In some organizations, this person may oversee just finance and administration; in others, they oversee every department. In manufacturing and retail, it tends to be very specific around supply chain, materials, equipment, and so much more. Regardless of where this falls for one person over another, soft skills and broad knowledge are equally important across all. When I help organizations hire for an operations role, I tell them that focus needs to be on the individual's ability to solve problems, be creative, and have superior resource management.

ADAPTABILITY: THRIVING IN THE FACE OF UNCERTAINTY

Uncertainty doesn't make curious leaders nervous—it motivates them. Instead of feeling threatened by the ambiguity of change, curious leaders lean into the space. If you are putting yourself out there, trying new things, and working to take things to the next level, you will inevitably get it wrong at times. The ability to experiment and feel comfortable with failure is key to being a curious leader and necessary for innovation, growth, and change. Curious leaders can become **effective leaders of organizations and teams that are also adaptive, agile, and ready to innovate.**

Curious leaders don't see failure as the end—they see it as the means. They are open to the fact that not every experiment will work, and they create spaces in which failure is seen as a stepping-stone to success. When people know it's okay to fail, they become more experimental. Incubating error creates an innovative culture in which teams feel motivated to **try different things, take risks, and keep learning through** their mistakes.

Reed Hastings, the CEO of Netflix, disastrously split his company in two when he put the DVD rental business into one company (named Qwikster) and his company's rapidly growing streaming business into the entity that would retain the Netflix brand. The Qwikster debacle instantly became a classic case study of how to learn from a failure.

The backlash was immediate and exacting. In the first weeks following the announcement, the company lost eight hundred thousand subscribers. Its stock fell by nearly 80 percent, a loss in market value estimated at the time at $12 billion.

The media were aghast at the move, and the customer base was equally damning, accusing Hastings of being clueless about customer needs.

Instead of justifying the decision or showing signs of covering up, Hastings simply said that the plan didn't work and took quick action to undo it. He extended the timeline for DVD rentals for the families that were affected by the plan, then issued an honest apology in a blog post that was highly unusual for a high-profile CEO.

Netflix made a brave move, and the gutsy CEO owned up to his failure and acted on it immediately. Most executives aren't as quick or brave to call for something so drastic, admit such a failure, then address it. Netflix's adaptability is seen at both ends of the spectrum in its willingness to take on the initial move to shake up operations and then its willingness to reverse when that move failed.

Reed Hastings's handling of the Qwikster debacle offers important lessons for leaders:

- **Make bold moves:** Making big moves helps when your growth is rapid, and it helps you keep growing.
- **Own your mistakes:** Hastings wasn't trying to shift blame or argue that a bad decision was the right one. Instead, he granted trust to employees and customers by taking responsibility.
- **Adapt quickly:** Hastings's ability to pivot quickly after recognizing the mistake was key to Netflix's recovery. Leaders should be willing to both adapt and change course when a strategy clearly isn't working and plot a new course when things are still working.

ASKING THE RIGHT QUESTIONS: THE CATALYST FOR INNOVATION

Asking the right questions distinguishes the most curious leaders. Rather than just seeking answers, the best leaders value inquiry over certainty because the search for the right questions helps generate deep insights. They also encourage their teams to ask the right questions by challenging assumptions, suspending judgments, considering alternatives, and thinking divergently. In the words of Albert Einstein, "The important thing is to not stop questioning. Curiosity has its own reason for existing."[4] It's that creative freedom that puts an organization on the path to innovation.

"Why is this process in place?"

"What if we approached this challenge differently?"

"What are we missing?"

These are the kinds of questions that curious leaders are constantly posing as they mine for opportunities to innovate.

When it comes to changing our lives, is there a more innovative product than the iPhone? Even though many smartphone aficionados of today grew up in the seventies, eighties, and nineties without a powerful computer in their pocket or purse, it is hard for us to think about our lives without them. The iPhone is arguably the greatest result of Steve Jobs's return to Apple after being ousted from his own company.

To bring out the innovation of the iPhone, Jobs did not begin with just answers and ideas. He raised the right questions. None of those questions were more impactful on today's phone than "Why do we need a phone with a keyboard?"

Starting with the right questions on the status quo helps break down what exists from what is possible.

Steve Jobs's success with the iPhone offers leaders important lessons about the power of asking the right question:

- **Challenge assumptions:** Don't take industry standards or norms for granted. Ask questions that challenge the fundamental assumptions of your business or market to explore new possibilities.
- **Unlock creativity by asking bold questions:** Encourage creative problem-solving by asking questions that push your team to look beyond the obvious.
- **Focus on the user experience:** When asking questions, focus on the end-user or customer. How can you make your product or service better for them? What questions can you ask to discover pain points or areas for improvement?
- **Open the door to disruption:** Ask disruptive questions that go beyond incremental improvements and push toward transformational change. Questions like "What would our product look like if we started from scratch?" or "How could we revolutionize our industry?" can help you break new ground.

I led a culture workshop for an organization that was struggling with innovation. There were also some personality conflicts and generational issues. I had them get to the bottom of an issue by only asking questions. I could see from her face that the VP was not a fan of this exercise. But once we started, she began to see how people were unearthing so many elements to consider in finding a solution through asking questions. The questions covered topics like value, marketing channels, customer engagement, and so much more. After the exercise concluded, the team committed to doing this exercise together once a month. The CEO was inspired to bring the exercise to the board at their next meeting.

SEEKING DIVERSE PERSPECTIVES: THE POWER OF COLLECTIVE INSIGHT

Diversity of perspective and input is built into innovative leaders' way of thinking. They actively seek out adjacent and divergent views on their work, inviting people with alternate perspectives to help them with problems, even if their views are not directly specific to the problem. Innovative leaders employ a broad range of inputs, working across different departments and teams, seeking answers from external partners, and even inviting viewpoints from unlikely sources. Seeking out diversity helps leaders consider the bigger picture of their challenges while seeing the problem with a new and clearer lens.

DEI (diversity, equity, and inclusion) has seen a whirlwind lately as many companies have gone from championing such policies and procedures to running from them. The social and political aspects surrounding DEI complicate this issue and distract from one of the key reasons it's beneficial for organizations—different backgrounds, cultures, education levels, etc., all help drive different perspectives. I once had a boss that said, "I don't just want employees who think, I want employees who think like me." There's obviously some nuance behind this, but having a team that only thinks the same is going to miss new and different solutions and ideas.

This also helps leaders see challenges with different eyes. A dead end from one angle might turn out to have potential from another. One reason curious leaders are better problem-solvers is that they tend to find solutions that are not available to others.

When Indra Nooyi took over as CEO of PepsiCo in 2006, the company faced significant challenges. Consumer preferences were beginning to shift away from sugary sodas and snacks and toward healthier alternatives. Nooyi realized that to remain relevant and successful, the company needed to pivot toward more sustainable, health-conscious products while also keeping its profitable traditional offerings intact.

Rather than relying solely on her own judgment or the advice of top executives, Nooyi actively sought out diverse perspectives from across the company and from external stakeholders. This approach led to the strategic initiative called Performance with Purpose, which aimed to position PepsiCo as a company focused on health, sustainability, and community impact while maintaining profitability.

Here are takeaways from her ability to seek diverse perspectives at PepsiCo:

- **Engage all levels of the organization:** Leaders should foster open communication throughout their organization, regularly seeking insights from employees at all levels. Frontline employees often have valuable perspectives on operations and consumer behavior that can inform strategic decisions. It is important to break down hierarchy and silos in each and every organization.
- **Embrace diverse global perspectives:** Leaders of global organizations must value cultural diversity and seek to understand the unique needs and preferences of consumers in different regions.

- **Balance innovation with core business:** Leaders must find the right balance between innovation and business fundamentals. Seeking diverse perspectives can help ensure that new initiatives are aligned with the organization's financial goals and long-term vision.

SEEING PROBLEMS FROM DIFFERENT PERSPECTIVES: UNLOCKING CREATIVE SOLUTIONS

Not just problem-solvers, curious leaders redefine problems. They are skilled at zigzagging through issues. They bring different lenses and frameworks to a challenge so it can be reframed in ways that expand possibilities. Instead of staying stymied on less-than-satisfactory solutions, these leaders use curiosity to go past the obvious, predictable strategies and brainstorm approaches others might overlook. With their teams, they can reinvigorate assumptions or approaches that caused the problem in the first place, then foster an innovation culture by pushing themselves and others to ask, "What if?"

When faced with a challenge, curious leaders ask:

- "How else can we look at this problem?"
- "What if we approached it from a completely different angle?"

A big part of looking at a problem from a different perspective is making sure you are correctly looking at the actual problem and not merely a symptom of the problem. An ability to even define the problem correctly is necessary to properly fix the problem as opposed to just placing a band-aid on the symptom.

Jeff Bezos told a story about what he calls one of the greatest contributions to Amazon. In the mid-1990s, when Amazon was still a young company operating out of a garage, Bezos and his small team were working long hours, packing and shipping books. At the time, Amazon was growing rapidly, and the team spent a large part of their day on the floor, kneeling to pack books and prepare shipments. Naturally, this took a physical toll on their bodies.[5]

The story goes that Bezos said they needed to invest in kneepads to minimize the damage to their ailing joints. A software engineer who was busy assisting with the packing turned to Bezos and said, "Jeff, we should get packing tables." Bezos got packing tables the very next day, and they doubled their productivity in less than one month.

This story showcases the importance of looking at the problem correctly, as getting kneepads would have improved only their knees and not their production. Tables did both—addressing the real problem that they were on their knees in the first place.

The story also offers valuable lessons for leaders on how to address problems through a fresh perspective:

- **Accurately define the problem:** When addressing a challenge, don't settle for the obvious or superficial problem. Take the time to analyze the situation from different angles and accurately define the core issue before jumping to a solution. This deeper understanding often reveals more effective and impactful solutions.
- **Look for simple, practical solutions:** Not all solutions need to be complex. Sometimes, the simplest solutions can have the greatest impact. Leaders should

remain open to basic, practical solutions that address core problems effectively.
- **See problems through the lens of process improvement:** Reframing problems as opportunities for process improvement can help leaders implement solutions that solve the immediate issue and lead to lasting operational efficiencies.
- **Question the status quo:** Leaders should consistently question existing practices and processes, even if they seem to be working fine. By challenging the status quo, you can often uncover opportunities for improvement that others might have missed.

"WHY AREN'T WE AMAZON?"

An organization and founder I had the privilege of working with helps highlight that even when intentions are good, growth and curiosity fail if you're not able and willing to go beyond your comfort zone.

I was brought in to help rebuild a service company after it had experienced several years of decline. It was a fantastic organization founded by a serial entrepreneur who is a wonderful person. The company had enjoyed an amazing track record and brand for years, but there had been a sudden reversal. One key component was a new competitor with a similar mission and value proposition that was cutting into the market share. After suffering a few years in a row in the red and having just laid off half its staff, the business was struggling and needed an operational assessment and a new course—my specialty! It was a dream engagement for me at the time.

I made some great changes in the business. It ended up in the black during my tenure, but many tough decisions had to be made. Some departments didn't have the skills they needed, while others were incredibly overinflated. A major shift in the culture had to be cultivated so the staff could move from a fixed, micromanaged mindset to a mindset of growth and curiosity.

The CEO was famous for saying, "We were founded the same year as Amazon. Why aren't we Amazon?" If you want to build an innovative organization of growth, there are few better examples than Amazon. So the CEO asked a great question. It showed that he had his sights on something higher. He wanted the organization to continue to grow and have a bigger impact.

But here is a story that explains why they were not Amazon.

That new competitor I mentioned did not have major differences except for the competitor's main content mechanism—video. Although both organizations had robust content strategies, only one was utilizing video content in any kind of meaningful way. This was not just some innovative solution. Instead, it was a well-known strategy to hit each business's demographics. I conducted research on the competition in an attempt to see if there were some changes we could make, and the only real difference I could find was the video content. That was the primary difference.

I brought the idea of launching more video content to our audience, a younger demographic. However, the CEO told me that was not what he'd had in mind when founding the company twenty-seven years earlier. Really? He didn't envision video being such a major piece of content delivery well before Instagram, YouTube, TikTok, and even smartphones?

To be fair, it probably wasn't really about the video content. I believe it was about several things that video represented:

- Feeling insecure about adopting a competitor's strategy
- Fear of change
- Resisting the source of the change—me
- A limit to the amount of change he was willing to accept—and especially from me.

Although he was an entrepreneurial leader and wanted to see the business grow, he was not immune to some of the factors that we have been discussing. The desires were there, but the mechanisms to continue to foster new ideas for growth were limited. Thus, so was the growth.

THREE SHIFTS REQUIRED FOR CURIOSITY, GROWTH, AND INNOVATION

Becoming a curious leader is not just about asking questions or exploring new ideas—it's about undergoing a fundamental shift in how you approach leadership. To embody curiosity, a leader must transform in three key areas: adopting a growth mindset, embracing operational excellence, and fostering a curious culture. These shifts provide the foundation for leading with curiosity and creating an environment where innovation, adaptability, and continuous improvement thrive.

From a Fixed Mindset to a Growth Mindset

The first shift is moving from a fixed mindset to a growth mindset. A fixed mindset holds on to the belief that talent, intelligence, and potential are static, leading to a fear of failure and reluctance to explore new possibilities. Remembering that our organizations are led by people and pick up their attributes, it is easy to see why this is an important component.

Think about leaders who believe they can get only so far or are just fine with where things are. In contrast, a growth mindset embraces the idea that abilities and intelligence can be developed through effort, feedback, and learning. It's the notion that we can push further and achieve more as individuals or organizations. As a curious leader, adopting a growth mindset means encouraging learning and improvement in yourself as well as creating an environment where your team feels safe to take risks, challenge the status quo, and grow. A growth mindset embraces learning from beyond yourself and allowing new ideas and perspectives to come into play. This shift empowers leaders and their teams to embrace challenges as opportunities rather than obstacles and dare to believe in bigger possibilities. Although a growth mindset is where the shift begins, it needs the other two shifts to complete the transformation.

Carol Dweck, an American psychologist and an expert on motivation, is known for defining growth and fixed mindsets. She aptly describes a growth mindset as "The passion for stretching yourself and sticking to it, even (or especially) when it's not going well, is the hallmark of the growth mindset. This is the mindset that allows people to thrive during some of the most challenging times in their lives."[6] A growth mindset is a combination of intention, motivation, and perseverance.

Operational Excellence

Curiosity should not be confined to abstract ideas or vision. It must be grounded in the way an organization operates. This shift toward operational excellence is about applying curiosity to every aspect of the business—asking the right questions, improving processes, and striving for efficiency and effectiveness. Leaders who embrace operational excellence view problems as opportunities to innovate, find better solutions, and continuously refine their systems. Operational excellence is about continually lifting every stone to regularly analyze and improve how the organization is operating. Instead of seeing operations as rigid or mechanical, a curious leader fosters an environment where continuous improvement is the norm. This shift positions curiosity as a driver of productivity and sustainable growth, allowing organizations to remain nimble and adaptable.

A great analogy for this is the concept of agile development, in which software companies regularly tweak and improve software to improve functionality and user experience while the app is active. Our organizations as a whole must operate in a very similar way. Organizations need to constantly be questioning, evaluating, and improving operations.

A growth mindset embraces learning from beyond yourself and allowing new ideas and perspectives to come into play.

There is an old saying: "If it's not broke, don't fix it." Well, I wonder how the leaders of companies like Blockbuster, Yahoo, Kodak, and Nokia feel about that concept. These brands were at the very top of their game at one point, but they became complacent and were unable or unwilling to adapt operationally to market trends. Of course, these are large companies with large problems. But, many organizations are being destroyed by small problems. After working with many organizations over the years, I've been surprised by the number of organizations that do payroll manually, handle expenses on spreadsheets, have paper onboarding processes, etc. These are very small components that have a very important impact on an organization's efficiency and effectiveness. These elements often involve an enormous waste of time and efficiency, but they also affect overall operations, morale, and retention.

I define operational excellence as an organization's ability to reach its intended results as efficiently and effectively as possible. That requires constant evaluation, questioning, and curiosity to ensure that the operations are being conducted with the utmost excellence.

Fostering a Curious Culture

The final shift is perhaps the most transformative: creating a curious culture. Having the right mindset and operational expertise are important. But unless you are the leader of a one-person band, bringing the team along with you will allow the organization to innovate, grow, and change. Without a team, the organization will undoubtedly reach a ceiling, at best.

> **A curious leader doesn't just lead with curiosity—they cultivate it across the entire organization.**

A curious leader doesn't just lead with curiosity—they cultivate it across the entire organization. This requires building a culture where employees are encouraged to ask questions, challenge assumptions, and explore new ideas without fear of failure or being reprimanded. In a curious culture, curiosity is not just a personal trait but an organizational value that permeates decision-making, collaboration, and innovation. Leaders must actively model curiosity and create systems that reward exploration and learning. By fostering a curious culture, leaders unlock their team's full creative potential, drive innovation, and create an organization that thrives in change.

Throughout my career, I, unfortunately, have learned more about culture from the negative than the positive. I have worked for organizations that do not fire anyone, which creates a free-for-all and low morale. I have also worked for cutthroat organizations, where everyone was worried it was their last day—every single day. That environment also creates low morale. Culture affects each and every organization's ability to achieve operational excellence.

These three shifts toward a growth mindset, operational excellence, and a curious culture form the backbone of a curious leader's approach to leadership. Together, they create the conditions for innovation, adaptability, and long-term success, laying the foundation for the detailed exploration that we'll cover in the coming chapters.

CHAPTER 2

SHIFTING FROM A FIXED MINDSET TO A GROWTH MINDSET IN BECOMING A CURIOUS LEADER

"Believe you can and you're halfway there."
—Theodore Roosevelt

Leadership in the modern world requires more than just knowledge, experience, or a title. It demands an openness to new ideas, a willingness to take risks, and an ability to learn from mistakes. At the heart of these traits is something even more fundamental: a growth mindset. In order to embrace curiosity and become a transformative leader, you must first shift from a fixed mindset to a growth mindset.

UNDERSTANDING FIXED VS GROWTH MINDSET

Before we explore how to make this shift, let's first define what we mean by a fixed mindset and a growth mindset. These concepts, developed by psychologist Carol Dweck, represent two opposing ways of thinking about intelligence, abilities, and potential.

- **Fixed mindset:** Individuals with a fixed mindset believe that their abilities, intelligence, and talents are static and cannot be changed. They avoid challenges, give up easily when faced with obstacles, and view failure as a personal limitation. Their focus is on proving their competence rather than improving it.
- **Growth mindset:** In contrast, those with a growth mindset believe that abilities and intelligence can be developed through effort, learning, and persistence. They embrace challenges, view failure as a stepping-stone to improvement, and are constantly seeking opportunities for growth and learning.

For leaders, a growth mindset is essential for fostering curiosity. Curiosity thrives in environments where mistakes are seen as learning opportunities and where exploration and experimentation are encouraged.

WHY LEADERS NEED A GROWTH MINDSET

To foster innovation and drive growth, leaders must adopt a growth mindset—one that embraces experimentation, welcomes failure as a learning tool, and remains open to new ideas. In a business landscape that evolves faster than ever, clinging to "tried-and-true" methods often lead to stagnation, while those with a growth mindset can capitalize on emerging trends, technologies, and strategies that keep the organization competitive. A fixed mindset, however, causes leaders to fear failure and resist change, restricting the organization's potential and adaptability.

Let me tell you about a small boutique retail company I worked with where the owner struggled with this exact issue.

This CEO had been managing operations the same way since founding the company over a decade earlier. He'd built a loyal customer base and developed a reliable, in-store shopping experience that worked well for the company's original location. However, as competitors moved online, customers began gravitating toward e-commerce, and the CEO was faced with declining foot traffic and sales.

Initially, he resisted the idea of building an online presence, convinced that his customers preferred the in-person experience. This is very reminiscent of the story I told earlier about the CEO who asked, "Why aren't we Amazon?" Each situation had a CEO who loved what was built but was resistant to changing the company's original plans. When I proposed setting up an online store, the boutique CEO's response was classic fixed mindset: "That's not our style" or "We've always done it this way."

But with time, I encouraged him to look at the data.

Our experiment? Set up a small online catalog with limited items to test customer interest.

After a month, the new website generated more engagement than expected and sales were showing promising growth from a mix of local and even out-of-state customers. Seeing this early success encouraged the CEO to experiment more with this approach. We tested email marketing, started a customer loyalty program, and offered free in-store pickup for online purchases. The results were transformative. Within six months, online sales accounted for nearly 20 percent of the company's revenue.

This CEO's shift to a growth mindset was a game-changer. What started as a small experiment turned into a powerful revenue stream. Embracing experimentation and being open to failure allowed him to expand his business beyond the store walls and serve a broader customer base. Had he held on to his fixed mindset, he might still be watching foot traffic dwindle rather than growing the business in new, innovative ways.

On the alternative, I met a prospective client that, let's say, was selling rare coins. Very niche market, but he had garnered quite the following. He ran his business online and specifically through social media. But it was all done via spreadsheet, bids real time—one at a time, etc. He believed this was necessary to keep the connection with his customers. However, he also wanted to grow. This very manual and individualized process was a direct contradiction to the growth he wanted. Unfortunately, I was unable to convince him that, like the other example, he can change the way he operates to create more growth and scale and not lose that touch with the customer. He chose to continue doing exactly what he always has, which kept him exactly where he always was and unable to scale.

These examples highlight how leaders with a growth mindset view change and experimentation as essential for keeping their businesses thriving, and those with fixed do not.

I have worked with many business owners, CEOs, nonprofit leaders, and even volunteers who get into the habit of loving what is instead of what can be. Early in my career, I had a very prominent person in an organization I was working for tell me I was ruining "his" organization. Now, keep in mind that I was not suggesting we change the mission, vision, or values of the organization. I was not even suggesting that we change the business model overall.

I suggested that we charge for the banquet in order to keep the event within budget. The budget was tight, so I proposed charging those who were not the intended banquet participants. This illustrates how resistant some people are to change and how significant an impact they believe it can have!

Thomas Edison's journey to invent the light bulb is one of the most powerful examples of a growth mindset in action. Edison's goal was ambitious: Create a reliable, long-lasting light source that was affordable and practical for widespread use. However, the path to achieving this was filled with repeated failures. Rather than seeing each failed attempt as a setback, Edison viewed them as necessary steps toward success. When asked about his numerous unsuccessful attempts, he's widely attributed with responding, "I have not failed. I've just found ten thousand ways that won't work."[7]

This response reveals a mindset focused on learning and resilience rather than the outcome alone. Edison understood that each failed attempt brought him one step closer to finding the solution. He saw each "failure" as valuable feedback, helping him understand what materials, designs, and techniques didn't work. Instead of being discouraged, he used each setback as an opportunity to refine his approach and make progress. This is also reminiscent of Winston Churchill's famous quote, "Success is the ability to go from failure to failure without losing your enthusiasm."[8]

Edison's approach exemplifies the growth mindset, where failure is not seen as a final verdict but as a necessary part of the innovation process. His persistence and openness to learning from mistakes ultimately led to one of the most transformative inventions in modern history—the practical electric light bulb. This invention changed the world and set a powerful example of how viewing challenges as learning opportunities can lead to groundbreaking success.

For leaders, Edison's journey is a reminder that true innovation requires patience, curiosity, and a willingness to embrace failure as part of the process. By adopting this growth mindset, we allow ourselves to explore, iterate, and evolve, ultimately leading to greater breakthroughs and long-term success.

LEARNING AND DEVELOPMENT FUEL LEADERSHIP GROWTH

Curious leaders recognize that they are not the final authority on all matters. They are open to learning from others—whether it's their peers, their teams, or even competitors. This type of leader understands that learning is a lifelong process, and it's what keeps them relevant and adaptable in the face of change.

With a fixed mindset, leaders may believe they have already mastered their craft and have little left to learn. They may believe that what they envisioned years or decades ago is still a winning strategy. This arrogance creates blind spots, stifling growth and curiosity. By adopting a growth mindset, you open yourself up to feedback and continuous learning, both of which are essential for staying ahead in a fast-moving world. Confucius put it this way: "If you are the smartest person in the room, then you are in the wrong room."[9] How many meetings and rooms have you been in where the leader drives everything their direction without giving ample attention to the other voices in the room?

Satya Nadella, CEO of Microsoft, embraced a growth mindset when he took the helm. Instead of resting on the company's past successes, he encouraged a culture of continuous learning and improvement, pivoting the company toward cloud computing and artificial intelligence. Nadella attributes Dweck's book *Mindset* as the source that helped spur his work to transform Microsoft.

Embracing a growth mindset, Nadella built a culture around continuous learning, experimentation, moving forward, empathy, and collaboration. He challenged his team to see failures as learning opportunities. Under Nadella's leadership, Microsoft went from being seen as a fading tech giant to being recognized as one of the most innovative and valuable companies in the world. And it saw tremendous growth in revenue and market capitalization.

Curious leaders must dare to be dumb! As an operations professional and consultant for small organizations, I was often the only person on staff who handled operational matters. Throughout my career, I have overseen internal operational functions as well as cross-departmental operations. In these roles, it is impossible to know everything about everything. But I had to know enough to know where to turn and be able to analyze, question, and strategize each area. I had to continually be willing to go to others

Curious leaders must dare to be dumb!

and rely on resources at my disposal to find the answers and get results because, quite frankly, it was all up to me. This requires a certain humility. To be quite honest, I would often even play up more ignorance (daring to be dumb) on the subject matter than there was just to help elicit more ideas and conversation.

Too many leaders are too arrogant to admit they do not know the answer or to openly seek it out. Being a curious leader who embraces learning and development includes being willing to admit we do not know, dare to look dumb, and do what needs to be done to find the answer and further our growth and knowledge.

ADAPTABILITY IS CRUCIAL IN A RAPIDLY CHANGING WORLD

In today's business environment, change is constant. Whether it's technological advancements, shifts in consumer preferences, or economic uncertainty, leaders must be able to adapt quickly. A fixed mindset, which resists change, will leave you unprepared to pivot when necessary. By contrast, a growth mindset sees change as an opportunity to learn and grow rather than a threat.

Leaders with a growth mindset foster adaptability in their teams by encouraging open communication, collaboration, and experimentation. This creates an organizational culture where change is embraced, not feared.

Netflix transitioned from a DVD rental service to a streaming giant and original content creator—a shift driven by a growth-oriented leadership team. It recognized early on that consumer behaviors were shifting, and it adapted by continuously innovating its offerings. Its ability to adapt quickly to market changes has been a key factor in its sustained success.

This kind of adaptability is similar to the concept of agile development in the tech world that I continually mention. I think it is a great analogy for many components of becoming a curious leader. In agile methodology, instead of rigidly following a long-term plan, teams work in short cycles, frequently testing, iterating, and refining based on real-time feedback. This iterative process allows teams to adapt their product or service continuously, responding to user needs and market demands as they emerge. In the same way, a growth mindset allows leaders and teams to treat their strategies and processes as flexible, evolving systems rather than fixed plans. By embracing a growth mindset, organizations become more agile and are equipped to respond dynamically to the challenges and opportunities that arise.

Leaders who foster a growth mindset encourage their teams to be adaptable and continuously learn and experiment, leading to an organization that is more resilient, innovative, and prepared for whatever comes next.

BELIEF IN ONESELF

Another core concept of adopting a growth mindset is believing that you, yourself, are capable of more. This belief might sound simple, but it's incredibly powerful—and often elusive.

Many of us know individuals, whether personally or professionally, who feel that where they are is all that they are capable of. But that mindset goes even further. These people hold on to a sense that what they have is all that is available to them. There's almost a sense of resignation, as if they are destined to go only so far or the universe has intentionally assigned them a finite amount of potential.

But here's the truth: More often than not, it's not a lack of ability holding us back but our own beliefs about what we're capable of. These negative attitudes get engrained into us for a variety of reasons, and they're natural. The key is to create mechanisms in our mindset that help us recognize and address these limiting beliefs.

As Henry Ford famously said, "Whether you think you can or think you can't, you're right."[10] This quote resonates deeply because it speaks to the very heart of a growth mindset—the shift from self-doubt to self-belief. It's not just about wishful thinking or blind optimism. It's about challenging the internal narrative that limits us, questioning the stories we tell ourselves about our capabilities, and recognizing that our potential is often much greater than we imagine. A growth mindset invites us to see every setback and every doubt as a stepping-stone rather than a stumbling block.

For me, this journey started with a shift in focus from external achievements to internal growth. I initially sought out a professional development coach to work on business strategies. But we more often ended up working on mindfulness, self-belief, and conscious presence. That shift was transformative. By focusing inward, I was able to identify the limiting beliefs that had been subtly holding me back. This experience opened the door to an entirely new approach to growth—one that I hadn't previously considered.

I dove headfirst into books and lectures by Wayne Dyer, Alan Watts, Eckhart Tolle, Michael Singer, and Dr. Joe Dispenza—thought leaders who discuss the power of belief, consciousness, and mindfulness. Their teachings illuminated something profound: Adopting a growth mindset isn't just about changing behaviors or setting new goals. It's about rewiring the very way we see ourselves and our place in the world.

Wayne Dyer often said, "When you change the way you look at things, the things you look at change."[11] This simple but profound shift in perspective reminded me that our external limitations are often a reflection of our internal ones. Many of these authors and gurus even bring in elements of quantum physics to show how powerful our minds and beliefs truly are.

The moment I began seeing challenges as opportunities for growth rather than obstacles to success, everything started to change. We cannot achieve more without first believing we can. We have to disregard our fears and limiting beliefs and dare to dream bigger.

One particularly impactful experience was reading Michael Singer's *The Untethered Soul*, in which he discusses the "voice in your head" that constantly critiques, doubts, and second-guesses. Recognizing this voice as separate from my true self was a revelation. By learning to observe my own thoughts rather than be controlled by them, I found myself able to push through moments of self-doubt. This practice allowed me to let go of that ceiling I had unknowingly placed on myself and instead embrace a mindset of endless potential. This is often a tough concept to understand for type-A, go-getter, successful leaders. After all, I had a successful academic career and had some great achievements in my professional career. So why did I still have self-doubt? Why was there that occasional voice in my head, and how could I balance that with being a confident and secure leader? It was important to realize that the existence of the voice is not the true self but rather a little blip that comes in and has to be addressed.

This shift from self-doubt to self-belief has also had a tangible impact on my approach to innovation and business. A growth mindset isn't just a personal tool. It's a foundation for everything I do. Instead of focusing solely on measurable outcomes, I began to see every challenge as a chance to learn something new. This mindset empowered me to take risks I might have avoided before, step outside my comfort zone, and embrace change rather than fear it.

Adopting a growth mindset is about constantly pushing beyond perceived barriers and unlocking new levels of success, even when that barrier is simply one's own mind. This journey is not always easy—self-doubt, after all, can be persistent. But with each step forward, the rewards are transformative. The belief that we are capable of more than we initially thought opens doors we didn't even know were there. It's the spark that fuels innovation, growth, and change—not just in our businesses but in every area of our lives.

When I was working with that aforementioned professional development coach, he would often say that he usually had to get his clients to do more. That was never my problem. In fact, he would often say that I needed to do less! My background, combined with my diverse skills and interests, makes me open to many possibilities and desires. But still, without the belief in myself, these goals and actions could only go so far.

Transitions really began once I learned to tackle my self-doubt and *fully* embrace the possibilities. The book that opened this wide open for me was *Soul Without Shame* by Byron Brown. My coach had a multimillionaire millennial entrepreneur on his podcast. This young man understood the consciousness and mindfulness elements so naturally. I just had to speak to him. So my coach connected us. After hearing my story and learning where I was, this young entrepreneur recommended *Soul Without Shame*. It launched in me a passion for even more personal discovery that helped me believe even more in myself, understand how and why self-doubt can still creep in, and, more importantly, how to stay positive and continue to move forward.

A growth mindset is the foundation for everything. It gives us the courage to challenge the status quo, see setbacks as stepping-stones, and keep pushing forward even when success feels out of reach. When we shift our mindset in this way, we're not just opening the door to external success; we're transforming our entire approach to life. Every experience becomes an opportunity, every setback a lesson, and every moment a chance to become something greater than we were before.

THE SHIFT: MOVING FROM FIXED TO GROWTH MINDSET

Shifting from a fixed mindset to a growth mindset doesn't happen overnight. It's a journey—one that requires self-reflection, intention, self-belief, and a willingness to get uncomfortable. But it's a journey every leader must embark on if they want to be curious, adaptable, and effective in today's world.

When I started becoming aware of my own fixed mindset tendencies, it was like looking in the mirror and seeing things I hadn't wanted to admit. We are all a work in progress. And even though curiosity is a very natural attribute for me, I still have to work on things every single day. That's why most entrepreneurial gurus out there miss the mark. Their mantra is that they are always batting a thousand, and anyone who isn't "is a loser." But the reality is that we all experience setbacks, failures, fixed minds, and self-doubt. The goal is to keep moving toward the growth mindset.

Acknowledge Your Fixed Mindset Tendencies

The first step is to recognize those fixed mindset habits. I had to ask myself some tough questions:

- "Am I avoiding challenges because I don't want to risk failing?"
- "Do I feel a bit defensive when someone offers feedback, especially if it's less than glowing?"
- "Do I avoid certain tasks or projects simply because they push me too far out of my comfort zone?"
- Do I focus just as much (or more) to where an idea comes from as opposed to completely focusing on the value of the idea?

When I am feeling static and things are not moving forward the way I want, I tend to fall into busy administrative work to make myself feel like I'm doing what needs to be done. But that's anything but the truth.

I think we all have those moments of doubt or defensiveness, but becoming aware of them is crucial. For me, it was humbling to realize just how often I fell back on a fixed mindset, even as I preached to my team the importance of growth. Recognizing these moments isn't always easy, but it's the first step toward embracing a mindset that's open to change, learning, and improvement. For any problem, first recognizing the problem is the first step in fixing it. Going back to earlier conversations about personality assessments, I see myself as a very self-aware individual. (Undoubtedly, my wife may disagree at times.) I'm constantly re-evaluating my mindset and my actions to ensure that I am not getting into my own way.

Reframe Failure as Learning

One of the biggest shifts I had to make was in how I saw failure.

Growing up and early in my career, I saw failure as something to avoid at all costs. It was something that marked you, a stain that couldn't be easily erased. But adopting a growth mindset meant rethinking failure entirely. And, of course, I had some bosses who did not tolerate failure, which helped reinforce a fixed mindset.

Now I try to see each failure as feedback that's part of a larger learning process. Instead of dwelling on what went wrong when something doesn't go as planned, I ask, "What can I learn from this?" It's a simple question, but it's a powerful one. It shifts the focus from blame to growth. I embrace just trying new things and seeing what works.

In fact, I introduced a lessons-learned session after every major project with my team. I'll be honest—initially, some people were hesitant. They felt vulnerable openly discussing what didn't work. But over time, these sessions became a safe space—a place where we could dissect not just our successes but also our stumbles. Slowly, I saw my team grow more comfortable with taking risks and experimenting. They knew that even if things didn't go perfectly, we'd all be learning together.

Seek Feedback and Be Open to Critique

As a leader, I realized I couldn't expect my team to embrace a growth mindset if I wasn't modeling it myself. So I started actively seeking feedback from my team—not just the polite, surface-level feedback but the honest kind that stings a little. I'd ask, "How can I improve?" or "What could I have done differently to support you better?" And believe me, the first few times I asked, the answers were hard to hear. But I found that the more I asked for feedback and truly listened to it, the more open my team became to giving it and receiving it from one another. We will discuss how and why this happens later on in more detail when we discuss culture.

Celebrate Effort and Progress, Not Just Results

In the past, I had a tendency to focus heavily on results. We'd celebrate when a project hit its target. But if it didn't, there wasn't much acknowledgment of the effort that had gone into it. I realized that this approach was contributing to a fixed-mindset culture, where people felt their worth was tied to outcomes. If they failed, it felt personal. As someone who has successfully turned around organizations by emphasizing results and metrics, shifting this mindset was a challenging realization for me. But I learned to realize that curiosity, knowledge, and progress were the targets, and by aiming for those, the results would come.

My mindfulness growth has also taught me that we cannot make things happen. We cannot cause results. We can do only what we can to bring them about. Then we just let the results come. There are always elements outside our control, so a shift to progress and effort is far more important than the final results.

Becoming a Curious Leader Through a Growth Mindset

Embracing a growth mindset isn't just about adopting new strategies. It's about making a fundamental shift in how we approach learning, failure, and growth. It's about moving from a place of self-doubt to one of self-belief and encouraging our teams to do the same. When we see ourselves and our potential as limitless, we open ourselves—and our organizations—to new possibilities, deeper insights, and continuous improvement.

This shift has made me a more curious leader and a more adaptable one. I'm no longer afraid of change and failure; instead, I see them as opportunities to learn, evolve, and ultimately strengthen myself and my team. When curiosity is paired with a growth mindset, we cultivate an environment where learning is celebrated and failure isn't feared. Instead, fear is valued as a step toward innovation and progress.

Curiosity and growth are inextricably linked. You can't have one without the other. To be a curious leader, you must first adopt a mindset that embraces challenges, learns from mistakes, and values every step of the journey. This journey is transformative, for both us as leaders and the teams we lead. When we embrace a growth mindset, we create a culture where curiosity and innovation aren't just encouraged. They thrive. And, in today's rapidly changing world, adaptability, resilience, and openness to growth are the qualities that set the most successful leaders apart.

> **When we see ourselves and our potential as limitless, we open ourselves—and our organizations—to new possibilities, deeper insights, and continuous improvement.**

JEFF BEZOS, THE RISE OF AMAZON AND BEYOND

Jeff Bezos exemplifies a growth mindset through his relentless pursuit of innovation, willingness to take calculated risks, and continuous learning. This mindset has been central to the rise of Amazon and Bezos's other ventures, including Blue Origin and *The Washington Post*.

Amazon's Growth Through Bezos's Growth Mindset

Bezos started Amazon as an online bookstore in 1994, but he envisioned it as "the everything store" from the beginning, showing his ability to think big and embrace growth. By constantly pushing the boundaries, he expanded Amazon into one of the world's largest e-commerce platforms. His growth mindset drove him to explore new sectors, from retail to cloud computing and artificial intelligence.

Amazon Web Services (AWS) is a prime example of Bezos's growth-oriented approach. Initially, Amazon developed AWS to meet its own infrastructure needs, but Bezos recognized the value it could bring to other companies. Today, AWS is a market leader in cloud computing and one of Amazon's most profitable segments. This expansion mindset was risky, as Amazon invested heavily in AWS despite it being outside its core e-commerce business. However, Bezos's willingness to explore and commit to this vision paid off massively, setting Amazon apart as an e-commerce leader as well as a technology powerhouse.

Other Ventures Fueled by Growth-Oriented Thinking

In addition to Amazon, Bezos applied his growth mindset to other ambitious ventures. His space exploration company, Blue Origin, reflects his belief in the value of continuously expanding human potential. Blue Origin's goal, "to build a road to space so our children can build the future,"[12] encapsulates Bezos's long-term vision and willingness to take on a high-risk, high-reward challenge for the sake of humanity's growth.

Similarly, when Bezos acquired *The Washington Post* in 2013, he faced skepticism about whether a technology entrepreneur could revitalize a legacy newspaper. However, with a focus on digital transformation, he applied a growth-oriented approach, emphasizing innovation, digital content, and subscription models. Under his leadership, *The Washington Post* expanded its online readership and regained profitability, showing that his mindset could successfully drive change even in traditional industries.

Impact of Bezos's Growth Mindset on His Legacy

Jeff Bezos's growth mindset has allowed Amazon to transcend industries and redefine what's possible in both technology and business. His ability to envision a bigger future, combined with a relentless focus on customer satisfaction and innovation, has propelled Amazon to success and positioned him as a leading visionary of his time. He continued to look for new ways to innovate internally as well as externally, which is what led to AWS. Through Amazon, Blue Origin, and *The Washington Post,* Bezos demonstrates that a growth mindset can lead to transformative change, proving the value of continuous learning, risk-taking, and expanding the horizon of what's possible.

THE DANGERS OF A FIXED MINDSET

Blockbuster is a story of a giant brought down by its own inability to adapt. It's a case that serves as a warning for leaders in any industry: No matter how big you are, clinging to the status quo can leave you vulnerable to the tides of change.

The time I have spent working with nonprofits, startups, and small businesses showcases that organizations can fall into this trap regardless of size and industry.

At the turn of the millennium, Blockbuster was the king of the video rental industry. It had thousands of stores across the country and was a household name. But even giants can be blind. When Reed Hastings, the cofounder of Netflix, approached Blockbuster in 2000 with an offer to sell Netflix for $50 million, Blockbuster's leadership dismissed it outright. To them, Netflix was a small player in the fledgling DVD-by-mail business and not a serious competitor. Blockbuster couldn't see that consumer habits were already beginning to shift toward convenience and digital accessibility. Its leadership viewed online rentals as a novelty—too niche to threaten Blockbuster's dominance.

That decision marked the beginning of its decline.

This story brings to mind an experience I had early in my career when I was working with a company that was reluctant to adopt digital tools. A developer approached us with the idea of using software to streamline one of our most tedious processes, but leadership dismissed it as unnecessary. They couldn't see the value, just as Blockbuster couldn't see Netflix's potential. We eventually implemented the system after a lot of convincing, and it transformed the way we worked. It was a lesson in humility for all of us—a reminder that sometimes, the biggest opportunities don't look like opportunities at first glance.

As the years passed, it became clear that Blockbuster wasn't just ignoring digital innovation; it was actively resisting it. While consumer preferences were shifting toward streaming, Blockbuster remained wedded to its brick-and-mortar model.

In 2001, it partnered with Enron to launch a streaming service, but the rollout was a disaster. Netflix, on the other hand, was already pivoting, focusing on streaming with a single-minded vision. Blockbuster's attempt was half-hearted—a reluctant nod to an emerging trend rather than a commitment. This was the hallmark of a fixed mindset: an inability to see digital as anything more than a passing fad rather than the future.

I've seen similar resistance firsthand. A client of mine once had a golden opportunity to partner with a tech company that could have modernized my client's entire customer experience. But, because the client's leadership was so focused on maintaining the current business model, they balked at the potential costs and disruptions. Years later, they struggled to catch up with competitors that had embraced digital transformation much earlier. Blockbuster's story reminded me of that experience. Sometimes, it's the reluctance to go all in on a new approach that leaves a company vulnerable to being outpaced.

Blockbuster also had another glaring weakness: It clung to policies that prioritized short-term profit over customer satisfaction. The company was infamous for its late fees, a policy that raked in millions but increasingly alienated customers. As competitors adapted to offer more flexible options, Blockbuster stayed rigid. Netflix, by contrast, introduced a subscription model that eliminated late fees altogether, creating a customer experience that was more convenient and forgiving. Blockbuster's inability to rethink its policies showed just how much it was stuck in a fixed mindset and unable to recognize customers' shifting expectations.

This scenario reminds me of a conversation I had with a business owner about customer-centric policies. Their return policy was strict to the point of driving customers away. I suggested testing a more flexible approach, but the owner was hesitant.

"We've always done it this way," they said, and I saw the familiar pattern of resistance to change. Eventually, we trialed a more customer-friendly policy, and the response was overwhelmingly positive. It made me wonder what might have happened if Blockbuster had been willing to ask, "What if?"

Even as a consumer, I see where a lot of businesses make these mistakes, especially when it comes to subscription models. Many companies try to hang on to every customer as long as possible, even when the customer does not want to stay, and there's not just a risk but a high likelihood of losing that customer forever. Any company that makes me jump over hurdles to get out of a subscription service will likely lose me forever. Let me use your service when it is of value to me and not try to get money out of me when it's not. I see this as very much a fixed mindset where we have our fees, we have our services, and that's it. Hanging on beyond value erodes customer loyalty.

There was a glimmer of hope for Blockbuster when then-CEO John Antioco recognized the need for change and attempted to shift the company toward a subscription model and online rentals. But Antioco faced an uphill battle. The board and much of the leadership were focused on preserving short-term profitability and resisted the very idea of transforming Blockbuster's business model. Despite Antioco's efforts, the company remained tied to its traditional practices, unable to commit fully to the necessary changes. It's a reminder that a growth mindset must extend through all levels of an organization. One visionary leader cannot drive change alone if the rest of the team is unwilling.

Reflecting on this, I remember times I've faced similar resistance. As much as I wanted to introduce new practices or ideas, I couldn't make progress because of entrenched mindsets in the organization. It taught me that a growth mindset isn't just about personal adaptability. It requires a culture of openness and a willingness to embrace change from top to bottom. One of the main factors that drove me to consultancy was that many leaders I worked with would not value the exact opinion and perspective I was giving until it was raised by an outside party.

In the end, Blockbuster's reluctance to adopt a growth mindset led to its eventual bankruptcy in 2010. Meanwhile, Netflix—which had leaned into growth, experimentation, and innovation—grew into an entertainment powerhouse. Blockbuster's downfall serves as a powerful lesson: In a rapidly evolving world, a fixed mindset that relies on established methods and resists innovation can be a company's greatest weakness. Blockbuster may not have foreseen the exact trajectory of Netflix's success, but a growth mindset would have helped it see that adaptation was its only path forward.

For me, the takeaway from Blockbuster's story is clear. A growth mindset isn't just about personal development. It's actually a lifeline for an organization. When we embrace curiosity and adapt to changes, we open up opportunities for transformation. When we don't, we risk becoming relics of the past.

CHAPTER 3
SERVANT LEADERSHIP AND CURIOSITY

"As we look ahead into the next century, leaders will be those who empower others."
—Bill Gates

In the modern organizational landscape, leadership styles that emphasize empathy, stewardship, and active listening have gained prominence and recognition. However, as much as these concepts have gained traction, there are also the **retractors who believe that ruling with an iron fist and having empathy involved is soft. Regardless, there is no doubt that a servant leadership style brings about a different atmosphere and culture.**

Servant leadership, in particular, prioritizes the team's needs and encourages a culture of service and support. This style contrasts with traditional, hierarchical models by placing leaders in roles that facilitate the growth and development of their team members. Successful servant leaders recognize the importance of fostering a work environment where curiosity is celebrated and nurtured. I believe that the notion of servant leadership is a precursor for taking the steps mentioned in the following chapters on getting to know your staff and creating a curious culture. To put this another way, it is hard for me to fathom someone being willing to take steps needed to develop and foster a curious culture without having the leadership philosophy (mindset) of servant leadership.

Curiosity—the desire to learn and explore—is a powerful catalyst for innovation and continuous improvement. It goes hand in hand with servant leadership. When leaders demonstrate curiosity, they inspire their teams to ask questions, seek new solutions, and challenge the status quo. By encouraging a culture of inquiry and open-mindedness, servant leaders harness their teams' diverse perspectives and creative potential, driving the organization toward greater adaptability and excellence.

When I think about the two stark leadership styles, I think about how different organizations are now from what they were more than fifty years ago. Today, the vast majority of employees work for small businesses. In fact, stats show that small businesses make up 99.9 percent of businesses and account for 46.6 percent of all employment.[13] Furthermore, manufacturing makes up just 3.5 percent of businesses in the US vs 25 percent fifty years ago and nearly 35 percent a hundred years ago.[14] I believe this is vitally important to point out because we are no longer working on factory lines, building the same part every day, all day. Our organizations are small and agile, and their employees have exposure to and are involved in multiple elements of the organization. This is why a more open and empathetic leadership style is important. This will become more clear during the chapter on creating a curious culture.

Servant leadership and curiosity encourage exploration, which can enhance team performance and organizational agility. These complementary elements can create a thriving, forward-thinking workplace through practical examples and actionable strategies. As we examine the impact of servant leadership and curiosity on organizational success, I invite you to reflect on your leadership style and consider new ways to cultivate a curious and service-oriented mindset in yourself and your team.

UNDERSTANDING THE PRINCIPLES OF SERVANT LEADERSHIP

Servant leadership is a philosophy that prioritizes the well-being and growth of the team over the authority and ego of the leader. A crucial element in this framework is the emphasis on curiosity. Curious leaders actively seek to understand their team members' strengths, aspirations, and challenges, fostering a deeper connection and greater empathy.

The concept of servant leadership was founded by Robert K. Greenleaf in 1970. Greenleaf introduced the term in his essay titled "The Servant as Leader," in which he proposed that the best leaders prioritize serving others, focusing on the growth and well-being of their team and community. Rather than leading with authority or control, servant leaders put the needs of their employees, customers, and community first, aiming to empower and support them.

Curiosity in servant leadership drives a leader to ask insightful questions and listen attentively to the responses. On a call one day, a mentor of mine reminded me that we have two ears and one mouth. Use them proportionally. This deep listening helps identify opportunities for improvement and uncovers each team member's unique talents and potential. Servant leaders create an inclusive environment where people feel valued and heard because the leader demonstrates a genuine interest in their team's perspectives and ideas.

Moreover, curiosity compels servant leaders to be open-minded and adaptable, guiding their teams through change with a proactive and innovative mindset. This willingness to explore new possibilities and learn from diverse experiences nurtures a culture of continuous improvement. It encourages team members to step out of their comfort zones, fostering collective resilience and creative problem-solving.

I am often asked about the leaders and mentors I have had. Although I have learned a lot from many people who were inspirational in my growth, there wasn't one particular leader I saw as the utmost role model. Instead, I learned from the good and the bad of each one of them. Even in my own leadership, I know there were times when I struggled with servant leadership, as I was eager to drive results and bring about change. It is important to keep it all in balance. I continually work to incorporate more servant leadership by emboldening those who work with me. Under servant leadership, there is the need to lower the ego even more and lean into the collective much more than driving everything individually. In servant leadership, it's much more about setting the direction and allowing the team to row accordingly.

In essence, understanding and integrating curiosity in the principles of servant leadership enhances the leader's ability to support and empower their team. It builds trust, encourages collaborative learning, and drives sustainable organizational success.

CURIOSITY ENHANCES SERVANT LEADERSHIP

An element of servant leadership includes curiosity and intrigue. Inquiry facilitates servant leadership by establishing an environment that supports growth and development, both for the individual and the group. Specifically, leaders who approach their role with a curious mindset will engage in more meaningful dialogue with followers, ultimately better equipping the leader to understand the world as others see it. The curious leader embraces the challenges and obstacles inherent in working with complex systems. This is a skill in itself since, as we have noted, when working with these systems, not everything is as it seems. Inquiry is genuinely invaluable. Furthermore, when a leader demonstrates interest in the thoughts and experiences of team members, primarily through intentional dialogue, relationships are strengthened, and those relationships fortify a culture of inclusion.

As curious servant leaders continually seek to learn and understand, they are more likely to see the need for development and better able to structure support to meet each team member's needs. This approach enhances an individual's performance while also helping the team reach its goals. A curious leader pays attention to team members' differences and identifies innovative strengths that will help the team address evolving needs, establish more effective strategies, and solve problems more quickly and in better ways.

In addition, curiosity helps servant leaders stay current with news about their industry and its trends, new technologies and advancements, and best practices in their field. This knowledge helps them lead their teams through change and difficulty and anticipate what might lie ahead. Servant leaders display their curiosity by asking the right questions and looking for new information and insights that add breadth and depth to their teams' work.

Curiosity enhances servant leadership by facilitating constant learning and creating a safe space for everyone to feel validated and appreciated. It creates stronger bonds within the team, helps people grow, and increases the leader's ability to drive sustainable success. Therefore, servant leaders should embrace curiosity.

I am reminded of the adage, "What happens if we train up our staff and they leave? What happens if we don't, and they stay?" I have always pushed for opportunities for personal and professional development. I encourage my team to try new things and be creative in their endeavors. I reject micromanaged strategies that enforce form over function.

Furthermore, servant leaders who display curiosity solicit feedback from their team members and adjust their leadership style accordingly to affect their team dynamic. This curiosity about feedback builds a culture of trust and openness where everyone feels comfortable giving and receiving feedback.

This curiosity leads to empathy. Curious leaders want to know how others see things; being curious helps them develop the ability to know if their team members are struggling with tasks or are feeling that they're not being attended to. It leads to creating a safe culture where everyone feels included.

Simply put, curious servant leaders are open-minded and welcoming of new learning, ongoing feedback, and ever-changing solutions. They are creative, empathetic, and ultimately able to spur change and lead teams to long-term success. Servant leaders who want to increase their curiosity can start by challenging themselves and their team to learn and think differently, fostering open communication accessible to criticism, and delivering that feedback constructively. They also adjust their approach to fit the moment's needs rather than relying on past strategies that may no longer work. Finally, servant leaders should continually put themselves in their teammates' shoes, which will help them gain others' trust and understanding. We all should strive to be curious servant leaders who value new ideas, innovation, and compassion within our teams.

BUILDING RELATIONSHIPS THROUGH GENUINE INTEREST IN OTHERS

Fostering close, meaningful relationships is one of the fundamental elements of curious leadership. In simple terms, it means caring. Suppose leaders start listening to their team members' dreams, struggles, and aspirations and ask themselves how they can make a difference. In that case, they see a deeper personal interaction than the impersonal workplace conversations that dominate day-to-day organizational life. Caring also fundamentally demonstrates respect and recognition, two of the most potent motivators. This is easy to say, hard to do, and much harder to do consistently. But any leader can do it.

Rituals and the simplest gestures of care can all create a sense of belonging and loyalty. For instance, a leader might celebrate the birth of an employee's child and the latest company-wide turnover rate. Other examples include remembering birthdays and other outcomes of curiosity and attention to detail; asking questions that touch on more than work; and creating opportunities for employees' ideas to be heard, even if not acted upon.

Furthermore, demonstrating authentic concern for employees can reveal strengths and talents they might not otherwise reveal, enabling leaders to use team members' diverse skills to better effect and thereby empowering them by confirming that their contribution carries weight. This kind of identification and encouragement helps place employees where they are likely to perform best. For example, you can use an employee's creative side to the team's advantage by giving them occasional leadership of brainstorming sessions. Or give an employee with quick data-crunching skills some of the more complex reporting projects.

People often develop innovative solutions or new ways of doing things if they feel their ideas are taken seriously and their views are respected. Leaders can enable this collective intelligence and trust by creating an environment where employees feel confident voicing their thoughts and opinions. Allow everyone to share their voice and ideas with respect and openness. Be curious and open to views; don't yell or belittle someone who says something different from what you think. Don't shoot down ideas.

In the end, relationships with a more intentional level of interest and understanding will produce a more supportive and collaborative work environment. There is a flow to these types of relationships that facilitates more effective communication, helps build trust and camaraderie, and makes it more likely that difficulties and conflict will have a positive outcome. For instance, a difference of opinion doesn't have to lead to division and animosity if the people involved have mutual respect and know each other a bit. Further, employees are more inclined to take on challenges when supported by colleagues. Even simple acts, such as seeking feedback for growth, become more accessible in an environment where there's a healthy interest in one another.

Building such connections helps leaders motivate, inspire, and direct employees toward collective goals and long-term success. It promotes a vibrant and flowing culture in which employees are engaged and utilized at their best. This, in turn, results in higher job satisfaction and retention. Indeed, continued investment in such relationships helps leaders build a resilient and high-performing team capable of great feats.

EMPOWERING AND UPLIFTING STAFF THROUGH CURIOUS ENGAGEMENT

Giving everyone a boost is critical to creating a positive and energetic environment. Since companies depend on people, tapping into their creativity is crucial. It starts with curiosity. Ask your team how you can empower them to do their work or ensure a better environment. Ask if they have any recommendations for improving the service or product quality. In return, they might ask how you arrived at a particular judgment or whether you were aware of something that just happened. This process boosts morale and frees up employee energy for other tasks.

> **Ask your team how you can empower them to do their work or ensure a better environment. Ask if they have any recommendations for improving the service or product quality.**

Curious engagement includes asking enlightening questions, providing helpful feedback, and encouraging lifelong learning. Leaders may ask employees what their career goals are and look for ways for them to practice or exercise the skills required for a future role. Employees feel seen and understood, and they gain confidence in bringing more of themselves to the team.

Besides developing each individual, curious engagement also cultivates an organizational culture of care and openness. When leaders show enthusiasm for their team members' growth, they model a mindset and behavior that will carry over to how people treat each other. The net effect is that employees become more likely to engage with each other curiously—leading to increased curiosity and innovation throughout the organization.

By investing in curious engagement, companies can reap the rewards of employee retention, including greater job satisfaction, better performance, and lower turnover. Interested employees are mobilized, energized employees who are more likely to innovate, speak up, act of their own volition, and advance their organizations. In short, curiosity fosters a dynamic, empowering work environment in which everyone feels empowered to thrive.

THE RESURGENCE OF MICROSOFT THROUGH CEO NADELLA

Although Satya Nadella was mentioned above, his ability and willingness to adopt servant leadership to foster innovation, growth, and change through curiosity are also worth describing. When Nadella took over as CEO in 2014, Microsoft was seen as a stagnant, bureaucratic company struggling to keep pace with competitors like Google and Apple. Nadella's servant leadership approach—centered on curiosity, empathy, and empowered employees—transformed Microsoft's culture, leading to a period of significant growth and innovation.

This mentality and culture had direct impact on Microsoft's success.

Focusing on Collaboration and Empowerment

Nadella prioritized collaboration—both inside Microsoft and with external partners—and broke away from Microsoft's previous siloed approach. He encouraged curiosity about customer needs and industry trends, which led to key strategic partnerships—including the integration of Microsoft Office on iOS and Android—and collaborations with competitors, like Linux. This openness to new ideas and outside perspectives positioned Microsoft as a more versatile and customer-centric organization, which contributed significantly to the growth of Microsoft's Azure cloud services.

Innovating with Empathy and Customer-Centricity

Nadella's servant leadership style placed a strong emphasis on empathy, encouraging teams to listen to and deeply understand customer needs. For example, Microsoft Teams was developed as a response to the evolving needs of remote work and digital collaboration. This customer-centric approach, informed by curiosity about how to best serve customers in changing environments, allowed Microsoft to capture significant market share in the collaboration tools space and compete effectively with other platforms, like Slack.

Driving Cultural Change for Sustainable Growth

Nadella's servant leadership extended to transforming Microsoft's internal culture. He introduced values, such as inclusivity and learning, to create a more engaged, diverse, and innovative workforce. His approach led to a period of sustained growth, as Microsoft's stock value tripled under his leadership, and the company became one of the most valuable in the world. Nadella's emphasis on curiosity and servant leadership reshaped Microsoft's reputation, aligning the company's success with its commitment to learning and innovation.

By fostering a culture rooted in curiosity, empathy, and a growth mindset, Satya Nadella's servant leadership at Microsoft drove a remarkable transformation. His approach enabled Microsoft to regain its competitive edge and become a leader in cloud computing, AI, and digital transformation.

CHAPTER 4
BECOME CURIOUS ABOUT YOUR STAFF TO MAXIMIZE POTENTIAL

> *"Leaders can influence and inspire others by getting to know them and help them reach their own conclusions."*
> —Paul Thornton

Your staff's potential is a vital resource, and understanding how to unlock it or get maximum benefit out of it is an essential management role. There are many techniques, methods, and approaches that will help you understand more about your staff and their strengths, weaknesses, motivations, what would remotivate them, and their longer-term perspectives. The more you know about your staff, the more you can help build a more dynamic, motivated, and productive organization. We will also look at creating a climate where staff can talk to you (open communication), build trust, and push themselves to fulfill their potential, take on more responsibility, and stretch targets.

Many CEOs, founders, and owners want to keep up a divide in an attempt to not get too close to their staff. After all, leaders may have to fire employees or make some difficult decisions.

Throughout my career, I have had very close relationships with some of my bosses, including some I would even call friends and mentors and believe many who worked for me have seen me the same way. I do not just mean a mentor in my career but also in life. Although that sounds like it may blur the lines, those close relationships allowed us to have very open and honest conversations when it was time for me to move on. There were no awkward conversations or hiding the fact that I was going on interviews. As my career advanced and I was building teams, I brought this openness to my employees and expressed a sincere interest in their careers in general—not just in their positions working with me.

Similar to the notion that servant leadership is a precursor to being a curious leader, so is the need to get curious about your staff if you want to be in a position to implement a curious culture.

THE VALUE OF UNDERSTANDING INDIVIDUAL STRENGTHS AND WEAKNESSES

Knowing the strengths and weaknesses of your staff—what each person is good at and what each should not do—is critical in maximizing your staff's potential. With a clear understanding of that potential, you can adjust your management approach to each employee so you can provide a platform for the best of their work to emerge. You can also assign work that matches staff members' competencies.

Based on knowledge of the team's potential, a curious leader will be more effective in maximizing what is possible, which in turn leads to greater productivity and job satisfaction on the part of the staff.

When you know your staff's weaknesses, you know why individuals should not be entrusted with specific tasks. Developmental opportunities can then be intentionally provided to help them overcome areas of weakness. This allows for a culture of continued growth and improvement. The adage in management and even in personal development was about helping people work on their weaknesses. However, there has been a switch from reducing focus on weaknesses to strengths and using them to the fullest. Let's take a basketball team. You have a six-foot guard and a six-foot-eleven center. No basketball is working with the guard on how to be the best center. They do not have the intrinsic characteristics (mainly height) to be successful. No, the coach is going to work with them to be the best guard possible.

Also, knowing what all this entails helps you identify coherent team dynamics while fostering cooperation. How? You can match complementary skills for mutual benefit, which can create opportunities for innovation and a stronger sense of team unity. It can help cultivate an environment of trust and risk-taking, where team members feel a sense of appreciation and fulfillment for their role. That makes them more motivated to excel.

One of the organizations where I was working as a change agent had a team that involved bloat and lack of understanding. In particular, there was a staff member who I truly felt was being underutilized. I believed she had skills and the time to do more. However, I was too slow to realize this and relied too much on her manager. Right around the time I had these insights was right before she left. I did not have the time to foster her growth and get more out of her. My suspicions were confirmed when in her exit interview, she stated that she was busy three months of the year and had to find things to do the rest of the time. Despite her manager being a micromanager, she didn't engage in a way that helped her develop and help the organization in a bigger way. The manager 100% believed in the employee and her abilities but lacked the curiosity to know how to use them best.

Ultimately, understanding individual strengths and weaknesses—both within each person and in their interactions with others—goes beyond improving team performance. It's about building a team that is stronger, more resilient, and more empowered to achieve both organizational goals and personal success. By valuing each member's unique contributions, teams can foster a culture of trust, growth, and collaboration that drives meaningful and lasting impact.

REVERSE THE VIEW ON THE YOUNGER GENERATION

There's no shortage of negative talk about the next generation. As a speaker, I have led several volunteer leadership trainings for large national organizations that address this issue. The average age of the chapter officers for these organizations tends to be over fifty. Of course, some organizations have a younger membership, but the officers often are well-experienced in their trade and have the time to volunteer as leaders.

Leadership succession and engaging the next generation of leaders is important for all organizations. It does not matter if you are referring to volunteers or employees. There are common threads when it comes to thoughts about the next generation: They are lazy, entitled, selfish, etc. Right? We all know the negative views about the younger generation. But here is a secret for you: The generation above you thought the exact same thing about your generation and the one before them. These views are nothing new. In fact, if you do a quick

Google search on "next generation quotes," you will see the same thing from the historic figures like Aristotle as you do with quotes from the twentieth and twenty-first centuries.

The issue of the next generation often brings up the discussion of how they "only want to do what they want to do." I hear this time and time again, and I talked about this issue when I was featured in a podcast and book. Getting to know your staff and what winds their clock seems like a new-age concept. However, two well-known business influencers—Andrew Carnegie and Napoleon Hill—were talking about this concept over a century ago. Carnegie's book *How to Own Your Own Mind* showcases their business and leadership discussions. In it, Carnegie explains how it is important to get to know your staff and inquire about what motivates them and what they enjoy doing.

I talked about this concept years before I knew about Carnegie and Hill's conversation, although the confirmation by such great business minds is certainly reassuring. It is important to remember that most jobs no longer involve factories, assembly lines, and the uneducated—as you have heard me reference before. The next generation of leaders and employees wants to be involved and contribute to the organizations they are involved in. The days of micromanaging staff are long gone—or at least should be.

The concept of being hired to do a job and doing exactly as instructed is not going to motivate your employees. Carnegie backs this up. Think of it this way: Do you think you will get more out of an employee who is doing 90 percent of what they hate or 90 percent of what they love? Put this way, it is easy to see that to get the most out of every employee, you have to get to know them and what they are passionate about. Having motivated, excited, and engaged employees brings more results, longer employment, and fewer mistakes! Getting to know your staff and managing accordingly should be seen as a critical element for staff retention and results for the organization.

Getting to know our staff and what motivates them is seen as a direct response to this view of the next generation. And although the next generation highlights this issue, it is important to see that this applies to all people in the organization. It is not just for the new and the young; it's important regardless of tenure, age, experience, etc.

TECHNIQUES FOR GATHERING INSIGHTS ABOUT STAFF

Understanding the strengths and weaknesses of a team requires curiosity, openness, and intentional effort. It's not something that happens by chance. One of the most powerful ways I've found to really get to know a team is by transforming performance reviews into something much more interactive and meaningful.

Traditional reviews with static metrics and checkboxes simply don't cut it anymore. Instead, these conversations should delve into what drives and motivates employees, offering insights into their challenges and uncovering areas where the organization itself can improve. I've used these moments not just to assess performance but to ignite motivation and uncover invaluable perspectives that improve operations. When I am conducting employee reviews, I am focused much more on the future than the past.

Another approach that has deeply resonated with me is conducting informal listening tours. Instead of structured meetings or surveys, I've made time for one-on-one or small group conversations where the goal was simply to listen. I've walked away from these sessions with a treasure trove of insights, often learning more in those candid moments than from any report. Sitting down without an agenda, asking open-ended questions, and genuinely listening has allowed me to connect with employees on a deeper level and understand their experiences, aspirations, and frustrations.

> **When I am conducting employee reviews, I am focused much more on the future than the past.**

Shadowing has also been a game-changer. Spending a day walking in an employee's shoes, observing their workflows, and witnessing their daily challenges firsthand has given me a unique perspective. Equally valuable is reverse shadowing—where team members spend a day shadowing me. This exchange fosters mutual understanding and breaks down barriers, creating a more cohesive working relationship. I still remember the look on a junior team member's face when they realized just how many spinning plates I was juggling. It was an eye-opener for both of us. The key for this is to make it fun and collaborative.

I'll take you back to an example I provided earlier. One experience that still sticks with me involved a highly capable employee whose potential I recognized too late. My gut told me she wasn't being properly challenged or managed, and while I had a nagging suspicion she could do more, I waited too long to act. By the time I had the chance to elevate her role, she had already found another opportunity. She confirmed my assumptions in her exit interview. She had so much more to offer, but she didn't feel seen. Had I engaged with her more directly sooner, I could have kept an amazing employee. That experience taught me to trust my instincts and act quickly when I see someone with untapped potential.

Personality and skills assessments have their place, but I've learned they need to be handled carefully. While they can reveal hidden talents and strengths, they should never replace meaningful conversations or real-world observations. I've seen these tools backfire when they create rigid labels, with employees dictating how they should be managed based on their type rather than using the information to foster growth.

Simple, informal interactions—like no-agenda coffee chats—have been surprisingly impactful. I've invited team members to grab coffee and just talk, letting the conversation flow naturally. These sessions often uncover things that might never come up in a formal meeting. Similarly, show-and-tell sessions, where employees share personal passions or unique skills, have revealed talents I never knew existed in the team.

Encouraging cross-departmental learning exchanges has been another eye-opener. When employees shadow each other or collaborate across silos, it fosters understanding, breaks down barriers, and uncovers opportunities for improvement. When speaking on curiosity and coaching executives, I often talk about how in today's organizations, every employee and every department has a unique insight and perspective of every action and function. Let's take sales, for example. Accounting cares about the receivables times, legal cares about the contract and promises made, marketing looks at ways to bring in the prospects, etc. Each has an interest in the entire process and how it is executed.

I've also implemented curiosity circles, which are small brainstorming groups where the goal is exploration, not immediate solutions. These spaces allow ideas to flourish without the pressure of judgment or immediate action.

Ultimately, creating an environment where employees feel safe to express their strengths, admit their weaknesses, and share their ideas has to start at the top. As a leader, it's on me to model curiosity, embrace feedback, and show that growth is a journey for everyone, myself included. I've found that when team members focus on their strengths while viewing weaknesses as opportunities for improvement, the entire organization thrives. It's about building a team that learns from each other, celebrates collective talent, and pushes toward shared success.

PERSONALIZED DEVELOPMENT PLANS

Individual development plans help employees realize their goals while contributing to the organization. The plans, which leaders develop by collaborating with team members, outline a specific route for growth—from strengths and weaknesses to a particular stretch assignment that aligns with career interests and likely paths in the organization.

After getting clear with an employee on their career interests and aspirations through a one-on-one discussion, the leader should work with the employee on identifying specific goals with timelines. These goals can be focused on learning and developing particular core skills, acquiring experience in areas where the employee could take on a leadership position, or preparing herself for a shift to a new role in the organization. At this stage, the leader and employee could also outline the preparatory steps that need to be taken—such as training, mentorship, or projects—to reach the set goals.

Check-ins should be part of the system. And they should be regular enough to ensure that the plan stays on track but infrequent enough to minimize distraction. The intent of these regular meetings should be to increase transparency and trust through feedback, celebrate success, and resolve problems or obstacles as the employee works toward their goals. The check-ins should also include milestones that mark the journey at pivotal stages.

Investing time and resources to develop personalized development plans for your team shows tangible support for their growth and progress. This, in turn, models a culture of continuous learning for the entire organization. These gestures help strengthen your bond with your employees and engender loyalty toward you and your company.

FOSTERING A SENSE OF BELONGING AND MOTIVATION

An environment of inclusion and mutual respect helps teams feel connected so they can deliver their best work. An atmosphere of inclusion encourages an exchange of ideas facilitated by appreciation and mutual respect. It celebrates the threads that make up a diverse tapestry across many strands. It allows employers and employees to cultivate a feeling of belonging.

Forming teams is essential, but inclusivity can be achieved through regular team-building activities, persistent team orientation, timely communication to keep a team informed, and celebrating the differences of its members. Approaches to inclusivity, therefore, nurture a sense of belonging in the workplace. Inclusive norms are often constructed through **establishing employee resource groups or unaffiliated groupings or by reaching out beyond individual teams when net-**

works are disconnected or at a disadvantage. To achieve inclusivity and a sense of belonging, employers can encourage or enable teams to make hybrid employment models work and encourage working parents to stay connected to the office until their children start school.

One of the simplest and often overlooked strategies from leaders is effectively communicating your vision for the organization, the project, etc. This is so very simple! Transparency and an insight into your thought process and goals creates an environment where the team is brought into your plans. Just simple communication can go a long way to being proactive and open.

> **Transparency and an insight into your thought process and goals creates an environment where the team is brought into your plans.**

Motivation can be bolstered. If employees' accomplishments are acknowledged and rewarded, a culture of learning and growth is fostered, and each team member knows how their work contributes toward the organization's goals. In particular, leaders should offer praise and constructive feedback early and often while facilitating professional learning and development and career advancement opportunities.

To execute on creating a sense of belonging and connectedness, organizations need to embrace technology to facilitate remote work or hybrid configurations, which enable mental flexibility and enhance intrinsic motivation. There is no shortage of software tools that many organizations embrace from project management software like Monday to communication platforms like Slack. The key is to ensure that it fits the needs of the organization, is embraced and utilized by leadership, and is strategic.

Mental and physical health can also play a role. Flexible work arrangements, fitness programs, and other wellness programs are essential to maintaining high motivation levels. This tells staff that the leadership care about their health. A positive and supportive work culture should help ensure that employees remain motivated and engaged in their work, contributing to high levels of performance and satisfaction.

You can also assess the pulse by regularly sending surveys and feedback forms to sensitize leaders to employees' concerns or discomforts. Once these issues are identified, it's vital to take early steps to alleviate them. Incorporating a feedback loop, which allows employees to provide feedback to their managers on their physical and emotional well-being, can help organizations demonstrate empathy and build trust with and among employees. This trust, in turn, creates a more loyal, motivated, and higher-performing set of teams.

CHAPTER 5
BUILDING A CULTURE OF CURIOSITY

"Curiosity keeps leading us down new paths."
—Walt Disney

Every chapter has begun with emphasizing in some way, shape, or form that the world, business, and society are ever-changing. Inability or unwillingness to address this change will inevitably leave you and your organization behind. As I mentioned earlier in this book, unless you are the leader of a one-person band, bringing your team along is crucial for success. Building a curious culture is the way to do that. As the rate of change accelerates today, no organization can afford to go without a culture of curiosity—one embedded throughout the organization.

First of all, it is important to address what culture is. Thanks to Silicon Valley and tech startups, I feel that many view culture as Ping-Pong tables, hoodies, and three p.m. fruit carts. Do not misunderstand me—those are all elements of culture but not the culture I am referring to.

I view culture as the traditions, behaviors, and *management* that dictate the organization's daily actions. So, yes, a fruit cart being pushed through the office falls under that. But I am referring to the actions that drive results. To say it another way, it is those elements that directly influence performance and outcomes. Management is often overlooked as an element of culture. However, how leaders manage and lead their staff directly affects the culture and the results that it brings. Can you think of a more important element that drives performance and outcomes than how the team is being managed?

Curiosity is a necessity for any organization that is looking to innovate, grow, and change. That is because curiosity is needed for challenges to the status quo and creative problem-solving. It fuels business agility. In a curious environment, people are expected to ask questions, discover things, learn new habits and ways of doing things, push back with constructive challenges, and be supported by their people leaders. Yet many are not expected to do any of these things. There is a tremendous opportunity to harness the potential inside your organization when all levels are curious, beginning with your leadership team. From the C-suite to your frontline staff, everyone must embrace a culture of curiosity.

Culture must be led and, in my opinion, led from the top. Cultures will form regardless, but when they are not defined and led, the culture that forms tends to be one we do not want. I have sat through sessions where the entire team comes together to define the culture. The problem with that? What if the team comes up with a culture you do not want to enforce and support? It will inevitably fall apart. Although we have focused on servant leadership and getting to know your team, that does not mean that you are not there to lead—and that means setting the direction. Defining the culture that drives results is a crucial part of getting there.

I worked for an organization that was going through a lot of change. To help with that, it went through a series of personality assessments. This was implemented before I came on board, but it continued with new hires and was a great idea in concept. In these assessments, colors are assigned to different personality types. A company committee even had some really neat ideas around it (so the team was brought into the execution). There were placards on desks to identify employees' colors, and an idea even arose to get everyone insulated water bottles in their color. I thought this was a fantastic idea. The problem arose with how the use of colors was implemented and became the organization's culture. Although the knowledge the assessments provided was intended to enhance understanding, employees used it to dictate how others could interact with them. To put it another way, the staff in return weaponized the assessments and the colors in a way that was not intended. Although I try to be a very open and empathetic leader, I am also very factual, straightforward, and even blunt. I would like to think I have a good balance, but I'm sure some would disagree. What resulted from these colors was not an understanding of how people are. Instead, it turned into a spirit of "You cannot speak to me that way because I'm a yellow, and I don't operate that way." This is why I believe cultures have to be defined and managed by leadership. Furthermore, activities around the culture should confirm the leadership's intentions and ensure that it is not following whims that arise.

> **Cultures will form regardless, but when they are not defined and led, the culture that forms tends to be one we do not want.**

I mentioned earlier that in today's organizations, we need to break down the silos and hierarchies. Creating a curious culture helps do that in a productive and respectful way. We will provide actionable strategies for embedding curiosity throughout your corporate culture—one department at a time, one person at a time. When organizations foster a culture of curiosity, they'll unlock the potential of their people.

CREATING AN ENVIRONMENT THAT ENCOURAGES QUESTIONS AND CURIOSITY

Creating an environment that encourages questions and curiosity is essential for fostering a culture that values learning, innovation, and continuous improvement. In workplaces where asking questions and exploring new ideas are welcomed, employees feel more engaged, empowered, and committed to the organization's goals. Such a culture shifts away from the traditional fear of getting it wrong and instead embraces the idea that learning is a continual process. It recognizes that curiosity is a driver of individual growth and a catalyst for collective success, helping teams discover new solutions, anticipate challenges, and adapt to change.

By encouraging inquiry and open-minded thinking, leaders create an atmosphere where all team members feel they can contribute, regardless of their role or seniority. When everyone feels free to voice ideas, challenge assumptions, and seek a deeper understanding, the organization becomes more resilient, agile, and capable of responding to an ever-evolving landscape. Here are some key actions you can take to cultivate this kind of open, curious culture that promotes both individual development and organizational innovation.

Creating a culture of curiosity in an organization doesn't happen by accident—it requires intentional practices and leadership that values exploration and inquiry. It begins with asking open-ended questions that challenge conventional thinking and encourage people to step into slightly uncomfortable territory. By probing deeply into a team's culture and processes, leaders can uncover opportunities for improvement and innovation. I've seen this in action during brainstorming sessions in which someone dared to ask, "What if we started over? What would this look like if we had no constraints?" Those moments of honest inquiry can lead to transformative breakthroughs.

Active listening is another critical piece of the puzzle. When leaders give their full attention to employees' ideas or questions and respond with meaningful feedback, it sends a powerful message: Curiosity matters here.

A colleague once shared an idea during a team meeting—something bold and a bit out of the box. Instead of dismissing it or moving on, the leader paused, leaned in, and asked thoughtful follow-up questions. That simple act of engagement made everyone in the room feel like their ideas had value. This is contrasted to immediately tabling the idea or shooting it down.

Organizations that thrive on curiosity also create environments where questioning the status quo is not only accepted but expected. Encouraging employees to ask, "Why do we do it this way?" opens the door to uncovering inefficiencies and discovering innovative solutions. Safe spaces for debate—such as regular team sessions dedicated solely to discussing ideas—can be incredibly powerful. I've been part of teams in which these spaces became the breeding ground for ideas that eventually reshaped entire processes.

Recognizing and rewarding curiosity-based outcomes is another way to nurture this culture. Whether it's celebrating a creative solution in a staff meeting or investing in professional development for someone who consistently asks great questions, these small acts of recognition reinforce the value of curiosity. I once worked with a team in which employees were given curiosity tokens to trade in for small perks when they brought new ideas to the table. It was simple, but it worked—it showed that curiosity wasn't just encouraged. It was celebrated.

> **Leaders must model curiosity themselves—asking questions, seeking feedback, and showing a willingness to learn. When a leader openly embraces curiosity, it sets the tone for everyone else.**

And let's not underestimate the importance of giving people time and space to experiment. Setting aside dedicated time for employees to explore side projects or research new ideas can unlock hidden potential. I've seen firsthand how a few hours of unscheduled time each week can lead one team member to develop a tool that streamlines a process, saving countless hours across the organization.

Finally, it all comes down to leadership. Leaders must model curiosity themselves—asking questions, seeking feedback, and showing a willingness to learn. When a leader openly embraces curiosity, it sets the tone for everyone else.

I once worked for a leader who made it a point to ask every team member, "What's one thing you think we could do better?" Those conversations sparked some of the best ideas

I've ever seen implemented simply because the leader demonstrated that curiosity was not just welcome but essential.

By embedding these practices into the fabric of the organization, curiosity becomes more than just a buzzword. It becomes a way of working, thinking, and collaborating. This kind of culture fosters a virtuous cycle of inquiry and innovation, where breakthroughs for growth and success are not just possible—they're inevitable. It is time to move beyond the buzzword and meaning of *culture* and actually drive cultures that drive innovation, growth, and change.

Why does a positive culture even matter? Well, again, I am not talking about fluff. I'm talking about creating cultures that drive innovation, growth, and change. These elements help motivate and retain staff. A curious culture is exciting to work for because it keeps things fresh, drives results, and allows for every employee to be a contributing factor. Can you think of better ways to not only retain your staff/team but keep them fully engaged each and every day?

ALLOWING AND VALUING INPUT AND FEEDBACK FROM STAFF

Creating a company culture where staff input is genuinely valued requires more than just setting up feedback channels. And contrary to popular demand, a curious culture that values feedback is the antithesis of a suggestion box. A curious culture establishes regular, meaningful opportunities for employees to share ideas and ensures that their voices are heard and acted upon. This means going beyond suggestion boxes and surveys. Instead, a curious culture builds a feedback loop that turns employee input into actionable change, reinforcing that their insights matter.

It is time to open dialogue.

I worked with a CEO client who was struggling to get valuable input from his team. He felt his team was disengaged and reluctant to share ideas in meetings. I suggested something simple but effective: Reverse the order of speaking. Instead of the CEO starting each meeting with his vision or thoughts, he let his team speak first. He also introduced a feedback forum after major projects that encouraged employees to freely discuss what worked, what didn't, and what could be improved. At first, it was slow—people were hesitant. But over time, as they saw their suggestions turning into real changes, they began to open up.

This approach did more than improve their processes. It transformed the culture. Employees started to feel ownership over their work, and the CEO saw a shift in his team's energy and creativity. One employee's idea about streamlining their project management process led to a noticeable increase in productivity. The CEO publicly recognized the employee's contribution, reinforcing the value of feedback and showing that the team's voices could drive real change.

In a meeting where feedback and ideas are valuable, leaders speaking last is an essential principle. I was working on a culture workshop prep, trying to address some of a company's issues, when I watched a video on Simon Sinek's book *Leaders Eat Last*.

That's when it hit me.

To get more employee input, it was paramount that leaders speak last. Now, I have gone on to learn that Simon Sinek stole this idea from me and is not regularly using it, but I'll let it slide. (I initially searched *Leaders Eat Last* to see if I'd pulled that from there, but I did not find it. I later watched a video in which Sinek used the phrase. I'm not sure who used it first, but I'm happy to be in his company, championing the concept and sharing its use.)

When a leader speaks first in a meeting, they skew the entire conversation their way. Unless you have already built a culture of feedback and even pushback, very few employees will likely ever go directly against the leader. However, when the leader speaks first in a meeting, those listening may be more influenced to apply thinking congruent with the leader's view, for they may feel it isn't appropriate to push back on the leader. Certainly, it is highly unlikely that someone will raise a thought or idea that is in complete contradiction with the leaders.

Speaking last allows the leader to create a space where everyone feels more encouraged to think freely and express their thoughts. As mentioned about culture overall, this is an area where leaders need to enforce and instill the culture every step of the way. Too many times, leaders adopt cultures but then do not work to instill them. You have to reinforce the concepts every day in how you work and operate. Directly communicate with the team that this is the new norm, reinforce it in every meeting, and remind them why you are doing it that way.

Encouraging managers and leaders to adopt active listening and respectful communication in response to feedback is essential. It builds trust within teams and between employees and leadership. Leaders should remember the principle of leaders speak last—a practice that encourages openness and diverse perspectives in meetings. If you can't stand the heat, better stay out of the kitchen. This is an important concept to grasp. The leaders and managers have to truly accept these concepts. That means staying engaged and listening—not grumbling under one's breath or vigorously shaking their head with every word.

Building a culture that values feedback isn't just about getting ideas—it's about creating a psychologically safe environment where people feel respected and motivated to contribute. Over time, this approach leads to better decisions, greater innovation, and a more engaged workforce. By systematically valuing and acting on staff input, organizations create a more fulfilling, inclusive, and effective workplace for everyone. I will be discussing this concept of psychological safety in more detail later in the book.

I conducted a culture workshop for a small organization in Washington, DC. It was having a few conflicts, and one of the main culprits was a generation gap. There were a few individuals under thirty, and the rest were around fifty. There were concerns about some overstepping, with the younger staff not staying in their lanes. I crafted a workshop that would help demonstrate how to create a curious culture and address what I was told was going to be the elephant in the room. Creating a curious culture helps resolve these issues from both directions—creating positive and respectful ideas as well as being positively receptive of them.

However, as soon as the meeting began, I saw some glaring issues. Although there were certainly issues of younger staff overstepping at times, I believed the bigger issue was how staff, including an executive, perceived things. I was shocked when the executive called out a staff member by name when the exercise was just to describe the organization's culture. As the session went on, I could see that the executive and another team member were driving a lot of the contention. This even manifested with these two individuals chastising several staff members for operating within an employee policy. It's clear there's a lot of shouting at the moon when you criticize staff adhering to policies that you are in charge of and yet do not like.

This goes to show how hard culture really is. When you bring in outside experts who put you through exercises, even uncomfortably, it helps bring out the real issues. The good thing about this organization was that it had a lot of positives in its foundation, but it certainly needed to do a lot of work to create a more curious culture that was driven by the top. When I reached out to this executive, as that was the one who hired me, I was informed that they did not like the workshop. I already saw this coming and reminded the executive that my job was to address the issues. Although I did not say this directly, as there was no need, I believe the real reason for the negative view is that it highlighted that she was the problem, or at least a big piece of the problem.

STARTING WITH THE NEW PERSON: FRESH EYES IN BUILDING A CURIOUS CULTURE

In most organizations, who generates the most eye rolls and backlash for speaking up?

The new person!

Why?

Because they don't know anything yet, haven't paid their dues, etc. Every person in that room or around the table is thinking, *You've been here for two minutes. What could you possibly have to offer? You don't know anything about this organization yet.* But in a curious culture, this is the wrong way to look at it. Fresh ideas and perspectives are constantly needed in a curious culture to drive innovation, growth, and change.

New employees, especially in their first few weeks and months, can provide invaluable feedback because they have the clearest view of inefficiencies, areas for improvement, or missed opportunities. The problem is that very few leaders have the courage and insight to tap into these employees' knowledge and fresh perspectives. Since they lack the biases or blind spots that long-term employees may develop, they are in a unique position to see what's not working—or what could be done better.

In any organization, a new employee brings something incredibly valuable: a fresh perspective. They enter the organization unburdened by the way things have always been done, and they possess a keen, unbiased view of its operations, culture, and challenges. In organizations that embrace a curious culture, this fresh perspective is seen as an asset—an opportunity to challenge assumptions and spark innovation. However, in more rigid or non-curious environments, the new person is often expected to quickly conform, and their questions or feedback may be discouraged because it's viewed as naivety rather than insightful inquiry. This is a significant missed opportunity.

Throughout my career, I have often been hired and consulted as a change agent. I love helping organizations grow. A hallmark of my skill sets and career has been my ability to step in with a new perspective and fresh eye to efficiently and effectively analyze an organization's operations to unearth hidden gaps, issues, and areas for growth. This was showcased at the start of this book in the story about my first employment.

Steve Jobs's return to Apple in 1997 is an iconic example of valuing fresh perspectives. Faced with a company that had lost its innovative edge, Jobs didn't just tweak the existing team; he brought in an entirely new executive team, injecting fresh energy and new ways of thinking into a stagnating organization. This new team, unburdened by the failures and limitations of Apple's recent past, was able to take risks, innovate, and ultimately turn the company around, leading to revolutionary products like the iMac, iPod, iPhone, and more. Once an organization is on a downward trend, it is natural for the leaders to focus more on not repeating issues that caused the downward trend rather than focusing on innovation, growth, and change. This is akin to making a bad financial investment. The last thing you want to do is throw more good money after bad.

> **Fresh eyes and minds bring fresh ideas.**

While not every organization needs a radical overhaul like Apple did, the lesson is clear: Fresh eyes and minds bring fresh ideas. You don't need to wait for a crisis to implement this principle. In fact, you can use this tactic every time there is a new hire, making feedback from new employees a routine part of how your organization learns, adapts, and grows.

BUILDING CURIOSITY THROUGH NEW EMPLOYEE FEEDBACK

New employees, with their unique backgrounds and unclouded perspectives, often see opportunities for innovation that long-standing team members might overlook. However, to fully leverage their insights, it's essential to create structured moments for feedback, learning, and cross-functional connection. By actively encouraging new hires to share their observations and ideas, you validate their contributions and enhance the organization's adaptability and innovation potential. Here are some practical ways to tap into the valuable perspectives of new team members:

- **Scheduled feedback sessions:** After an employee's first thirty, sixty, and ninety days, schedule a feedback session where they are invited to share their observations about the organization, processes, and potential areas for improvement.
- **Onboarding with curiosity in mind:** During onboarding, encourage new employees to ask, "Why?" and "What if?" about the things they observe. Let them know that curiosity is not only welcomed but expected.
- **New-hire mentorship:** Pair new hires with a mentor from a different department or role. This fosters cross-functional learning and ensures that the new hire's fresh ideas are shared with a wider audience in the organization.

Welcoming new perspectives is about more than simply hiring fresh talent. It's also about fostering a culture where every voice, especially those new to the team, is valued and heard. By incorporating feedback sessions, encouraging curiosity during onboarding, and connecting new hires with mentors, organizations create pathways for new employees to share their ideas and insights openly. Bake these mechanisms into how the organization operates. Once again, it is about being intentional.

Reflecting on my own career, when I was a new hire eager to make my mark, the confidence that my executives, managers, and even board members had in me gave me the confidence to continue to push for more change and innovation in my role. I also remember when I was a philosophy major in college. I had some thoughts after a class and emailed the professor. After he acknowledged the insight, he scolded me. He reminded me that these kinds of insights are necessary to help everyone learn, grow, and get the most out of the materials. He stated that I had deprived others by not sharing my thoughts in class. Although it may sound harsh, he was right. I have carried this lesson with me, remembering it when it's time to speak up to share ideas as an employee and when it's time to foster that confidence in others as a leader and manager. It is important to create the environment where everyone feels inspired and welcome to share their unique ideas for the benefit of the whole.

This process captures valuable feedback from new employees and sends a clear message that curiosity is a core value of the organization. New employees should know from the beginning that their perspective is both valued and critical to the organization's continuous improvement.

BEYOND THE NEW HIRE: CREATING A CURIOUS CULTURE FOR EVERYONE

Although the new hire example amplifies these concepts, they do not just stop there. Building a creative culture and implementing strategies are necessary for the entire staff to truly operate with a curious culture.

In my early days with one organization, I noticed how much change I was bringing with some very basic observations and fresh perspectives, which was great. But it also was evidence that the organization had stopped being inquisitive. It had become a machine with SOPs (standard operating procedures), micromanagement, and lack of curiosity. Curiosity needed to be infused throughout the entire staff. I realized that building a culture where everyone felt empowered to ask questions, challenge processes, and share their ideas wasn't a one-time initiative. It needed to be woven into the fabric of everyday work life.

So, one of the first things we tried was establishing regular feedback opportunities. I suggested quarterly brainstorming sessions in which managers and staff would talk not about their wins and losses but about how things were truly working. Our goal was simple: to make sure every employee was heard, especially those who might not feel comfortable speaking up directly.

To my surprise, people from every department started contributing thoughtful, practical ideas. We even ran a few anonymous surveys, uncovering suggestions that might otherwise have stayed hidden.

Regardless of how intentional you are in building a curious culture, there is no doubt that there will always be some who are just not comfortable expressing their ideas in large groups. Small, more intimate settings must be put in place to ensure that every voice is being heard.

One of the best parts was finding ways to celebrate curiosity in the organization. When someone proposed a new way to streamline a process or asked a question that made us reconsider an outdated practice, we highlighted it. In our monthly meetings, I made it a point to call out these contributions, sharing the impact they had and emphasizing that curiosity was more than welcome—it was a core strength. As we celebrated these behaviors, I noticed a ripple effect: Other employees started coming forward, willing to experiment, ask tough questions, and push for improvement.

Another approach that brought curiosity to life was encouraging cross-department collaboration. For example, pairing operations staff with people from marketing opened up new insights on how our messaging could better align with service delivery. Employees began to develop a curiosity-driven understanding of how different areas of the organization connected, and as they shared insights, we saw a surge in creative solutions that benefited the whole team. It was incredible to see how a small change in perspective could make a big difference.

Of course, all of this worked only because leadership, myself included, made it a priority to model curiosity. I made a point of openly asking questions, seeking feedback from employees at all levels, and even sharing moments when I didn't have the answer. Watching leaders engage this way gave others permission to do the same. I found that this consistent modeling was one of the most powerful tools for cultivating a culture of curiosity and creating a space where everyone felt their ideas mattered.

This experience taught me that building a curious culture isn't a quick fix. Instead, it's a continuous, intentional effort. But when everyone, from the newest hire to the most senior leaders, is encouraged to question, explore, and suggest improvements, the organization becomes stronger, more adaptable, and better equipped to innovate.

OVERCOMING NON-CURIOUS ENVIRONMENTS

I'll never forget when I was hired as a consultant for the competitor of an organization I'd worked for in the past. I adopted some strategies that I felt could help boost revenue, and the founder loved them. I was quickly passed down to one of his staff members, where the reception was not as warm. I got the sense that, by implementing simple and impactful ideas, I was stepping on her toes. She was very skeptical. It was obvious in how she responded to me at times and even found a way to sideline me at one point while still running with my strategy.

Eventually, the founder and I realized what was going on. Fortunately, the strategies that the organization implemented ended up helping increase its new market growth by ten times over in months instead of years.

This experience taught me a lot about how some environments, unintentionally or not, discourage curiosity and new ideas. In these places, questioning the status quo can feel like a challenge to authority. Conformity is quietly valued over innovation, and mistakes are viewed as failures rather than learning experiences. For junior employees or new hires, the ladder of hierarchy can seem insurmountable, with ideas rarely flowing upward. In an environment like this, curiosity can feel risky, and the energy that new people bring quickly fizzles out.

Reflecting on those early experiences made me realize how critical it is for leaders to actively create psychological safety—a space where everyone feels comfortable speaking up without fear of judgment or backlash. I began to understand that fostering curiosity has to go beyond good intentions. These cultural barriers need to be addressed head-on. Leaders need to model curiosity themselves, show vulnerability in not having all the answers, and invite others to join them in exploring new ideas.

I've seen firsthand the difference it makes when organizations embed curiosity into their cultures. When questions, exploration, and innovation are encouraged from every level, new employees don't feel like outsiders challenging the status quo. Instead, they feel like vital contributors, and they're energized to help the organization evolve. It's not just about making room for new perspectives. It's about creating an environment where curiosity is valued as a key driver of growth and change.

The lesson is clear: It's not just about tolerating new perspectives. It's about creating an environment where curiosity is celebrated as a cornerstone of success. When organizations embrace this mindset, they unlock their full potential for growth, innovation, and change. As a leader, you have to be intentional in breaking down the barriers that exist to curiosity and building a curious culture.

THE LONG-TERM PAYOFF

Integrating curiosity into the onboarding process and fostering an environment where employees feel empowered to question and contribute can lead to remarkable long-term payoffs for an organization.

I once worked for a cutting-edge technology company that was passionate about embedding curiosity into every layer of its culture. From day one, new hires were encouraged to ask "Why?" at every step and to bring their unique perspectives to the table.

One specific instance stands out. We had just brought on a new engineer who, within her first week, questioned a feature we'd been using for months with no real issues. At first, some team members were taken aback—after all, this was something they'd always done a certain way. But her curiosity sparked a deep dive into the feature, and we realized her perspective highlighted a significant opportunity for improvement. Her fresh insight ultimately led to a new approach that saved both time and resources in our product development process.

This experience taught me that when employees, both new and tenured, are empowered to stay curious and question established norms, the organization becomes inherently more adaptable, innovative, and forward-thinking. Over time, curiosity becomes the driving force that keeps the company on the cutting edge. It builds a culture where people feel comfortable challenging the status quo, knowing their perspectives are valued. And in a rapidly evolving tech landscape, this mindset isn't just a bonus—it's the foundation for long-term success and sustained growth.

There is no better mechanism for creating long-term innovation, growth, and change than empowering all staff, regardless of tenure, to speak up. I am reminded of the saying often heard in metro areas, "See something, say something." That needs to be the mantra of all organizations looking to continue to innovate, grow, and change. If you have a question or a suggestion that can be used to improve the organization, speak up.

INTEGRATING CURIOSITY INTO ORGANIZATIONAL VALUES AND PRACTICES

Curiosity is essential for much of the innovation, growth, and learning that can take place in an organization and can be integrated into not just a company's mission and vision statements but the day-to-day practices as well.

People need to feel that their employers encourage them to be curious. This means building a culture that prizes continuous **learning. And that means offering employees regular work**shops or cross-departmental projects, facilitating access to a broad range of educational resources, and making managers accessible for face-to-face conversations where individuals can discuss fresh ideas.

Rewarding curiosity-driven behaviors can also help put curiosity on the organization's radar. Company-sponsored curiosity awards can help put curiosity's value front and center. These can be open to any employee with a novel idea for the organization. We've also seen companies create areas in the physical workspace to display the innovative ideas of an individual employee or to recognize how that employee is **using curiosity to solve problems. Another option is offering** employees dedicated time to work on innovative ideas and bring them to a dedicated forum.

A much-needed caveat on developing values is to ensure that they actually exist. Throughout my career, I have run into two organizations that loved to hammer home *integrity* as a part of their values. Staff would repeat this word with such vigor and use it relentlessly when vetting potential hires and vendors. But, when it came down to tough decisions, I believe integrity would often go out the window.

With curiosity baked into organizational values and practices, businesses apply the power of the group, make it possible to continuously improve, and keep ahead of competitors that are being undermined by their own passive marketing and HR policies. By triggering curiosity, business owners create a work environment where people are involved, happy, and, at the same time, ready to face whatever the future will throw at them.

MEASURING AND CELEBRATING CURIOSITY-DRIVEN SUCCESSES

There are two complementary angles for measuring the success of a curiosity-driven program: quantitative and qualitative. Quantitative approaches help you track key metrics to show how curiosity leads to broader agenda-driven benefits to the organization. Qualitative techniques provide information about the impact of curiosity, which you and others in your company can detect and appreciate.

The first step in quantitative measurement is to start with a set of goals, ideally ones that directly tie back to your organization's broader goals. These goals are increased innovation rates, employee engagement, and successful implementation of new processes and technologies. Then, you need to regularly track progress toward those goals, proving the tangible benefits of an agenda driven by curiosity. Tracking will often involve some form of key performance indicators (KPIs).

Employee feedback is also helpful: You can survey staff about curiosity-driven initiatives so you can understand how efforts to stimulate curiosity are going down. Feedback sessions can allow staff to share their experiences and articulate what is working and what is not. As the relationship between curiosity and action becomes clearer, businesses can target their future initiatives to maximize the positive impact of curiosity on results.

Highlighting the successes is critical for keeping such momentum and encouraging a workplace with a taste for curiosity. Publicly recognizing these successes through company-wide announcements, awards, or other events adds to the rewards that can be gained from being curious. Public official stories about successful curiosity can be reported in the organization through newsletters or intranet postings.

The systematic quantification and highlighting of curiosity-driven successes doesn't just signal that a company's investment in this vital asset is well-placed. It also helps create a culture in which people are more engaged, innovative, and future-minded. This will help keep the company agile and competitive in a constantly shifting business landscape.

CURIOSITY TIPS: USE IMPROV IN BRAINSTORMING SESSIONS

A great way to foster curiosity and spark innovation in meetings is to incorporate improv exercises into brainstorming sessions. Improv, short for *improvisational theater*, operates under a few simple rules that can dramatically shift the way teams generate ideas, solve problems, and collaborate. The key rule of improv that applies directly to curious leadership and brainstorming is the "Yes, and . . ." principle.

The basis of curiosity leadership and the principles of improv are summarized in a famous episode of *Ted Lasso* where Ted states, "Be curious, not judgmental."[15]

The Rules of Improv and Why They Work

1. Say, "Yes, and . . ."

- In improv, participants are taught to never reject an idea outright. Instead of saying no or shutting down suggestions, you respond with "Yes, and . . ." This means you accept the idea presented, then build upon it by adding your own contribution. This approach prevents the stifling of creative thinking and allows ideas to flow freely without fear of immediate criticism.
- **How this translates into brainstorming:** When team members propose an idea, instead of focusing on why it won't work, everyone responds with "Yes, and . . ." This encourages additional ideas, refinements, or innovations. It also helps overcome the instinct to shoot down ideas and opens up pathways for new and unexpected solutions to emerge.

2. Avoid judgment

- In improv, all ideas are valid in the moment. There is no bad idea; the goal is to see where the conversation

or scene goes. This mindset encourages a risk-taking atmosphere where participants are less afraid of failure.
- **How this translates into brainstorming:** By postponing judgment, teams can entertain all possibilities, even those that seem unconventional or impractical at first. In a curious culture, this type of thinking often leads to breakthrough innovations or solutions that would otherwise be dismissed too early.

3. Build on each other's ideas:

- In improv, actors are constantly building on what their partners introduce. This creates a collaborative environment where everyone contributes to the scene's success.
- **How this translates into brainstorming:** In a curious organization, employees can build on one another's suggestions, creating a snowball effect of ideas. One small spark from one person can lead to significant innovations when the whole team is involved in expanding and improving upon the original thought.

How Improv Leads to Innovation, Growth, and Change:

By fostering a "Yes, and . . ." mentality in your brainstorming sessions, you create a space where new and fresh ideas are welcomed and nurtured. This openness leads to more innovative solutions because ideas are not immediately shut down due to perceived flaws or risks. Instead, they are explored, refined, and enhanced collaboratively.

Moreover, when team members know their contributions won't be dismissed, they feel more engaged and empowered to speak up. This drives innovation and contributes to a culture of continuous improvement and growth. Over time, this approach can lead to transformative organizational changes, as employees are encouraged to think creatively and take ownership of the collective brainstorming process.

Actionable tip: In your next meeting, try a ten-minute improv brainstorming session. Start with a problem, and challenge the team to use only "Yes, and . . ." responses to build on each other's ideas. You'll be surprised at how quickly the group will develop a range of solutions that might never have surfaced in a traditional meeting.

I conducted a culture workshop for an organization and had the team members perform this exercise. As I was explaining it to them, I could see the displeasure and distrust. But once they got the hang of it, they saw that it bred creativity, new ideas, and even some good laughs.

By embracing the principles of improv, you create an environment where curiosity thrives, leading to more significant innovation, growth, and positive change.

THE FOUNDATION OF PSYCHOLOGICAL SAFETY

A curious culture—one where employees feel empowered to ask questions, take risks, challenge assumptions, and share innovative ideas—can thrive only when it is built on a foundation of psychological safety. Psychological safety, in its simplest form, refers to an environment where individuals feel safe to express themselves, contribute their ideas, and make mistakes without fear of judgment or reprisal. Much of what I have been discussing about creating a curious culture relates to the concept of psychological safety. When employees feel psychologically safe, they are more likely to engage in behaviors that promote curiosity and innovation. They are more likely to speak up and not deprive others of their thoughts, insights, and ideas. This core principle ties directly to key leadership practices, such as getting to know your staff, accepting failure, fostering development, and listening actively.

Psychological safety is a critical part of creating a curious culture. As you think about elements of expressing ideas, feeling comfortable, taking risks, and allowing failure, it is easy to see why psychological safety is and must be a key component in organizations looking to create a curiosity to drive innovation, growth, and change.

The Aristotle Project: What It Was and Why It Mattered

In 2012, Google embarked on a large-scale research study known as Project Aristotle to determine why some teams outperformed others. Google, like many organizations, wanted to understand the dynamics behind its most successful teams so it could replicate those factors across the company. The goal was to identify what made a team effective—whether it was individual talent, team composition, or a specific set of practices that differentiated high-performing teams.

The research involved analyzing over a hundred and eighty teams across the company by collecting data from team interactions, surveys, and performance metrics. At first, the researchers expected that the best teams would be those with the most talented employees or the clearest structure. However, after years of analysis, they discovered something surprising: A team's success had less to do with individual talent or strict management practices and more to do with the quality of the social dynamics within the team.

The Key Finding: Psychological Safety

Among all the variables studied, psychological safety emerged as the most critical factor in team performance. Google found that teams with high levels of psychological safety were far more likely to be successful, innovative, and collaborative. In teams where members felt safe to express their ideas and make mistakes, productivity soared and innovation flourished.

Psychological safety allowed team members to:

- **Speak up without fear:** Employees felt comfortable sharing unconventional ideas or challenging the status quo without worrying about being embarrassed or penalized.
- **Take risks:** Teams with psychological safety were more likely to engage in risk-taking behaviors, which is essential for innovation and problem-solving.
- **Admit mistakes:** In high-performing teams, failure was seen as part of the learning process. Admitting mistakes and learning from them was encouraged, which allowed the team to move forward without blame or fear.
- **Offer and seek feedback:** Teams felt comfortable providing and receiving constructive feedback, leading to continuous learning and improvement.

The project revealed that when team members felt safe, they were more likely to ask questions, share their thoughts, and explore new ways of solving problems—behaviors that are the foundation of a curious and innovative culture.

Building Psychological Safety for a Curious Culture

Creating a curious culture begins with building psychological safety. As demonstrated by Google's Aristotle Project, the success of any team depends on the social environment leaders create. By fostering psychological safety, curious leaders unlock the full potential of their teams—allowing them to ask questions, experiment without fear, learn continuously, and contribute their best ideas.

By embedding psychological safety into your leadership approach, you create a space where curiosity can thrive. This foundation supports individual development and the collective intelligence and creativity of the entire organization. As leaders embrace psychological safety, they build a culture that exemplifies curiosity, collaboration, and innovation at every level.

CHAPTER 6

EVALUATING OPERATIONS FOR EXCELLENCE

"A leader's job is to look into the future and see the organization not as it is, but as it should be."
—Jack Welch

The shift to focusing on operational excellence is a key element of a curious leader as they constantly thrive to improve their operations to drive results.

Interrogating organizational operations is an essential leadership skill in today's complex organization environment. To drive growth, innovation, and change, leaders must critically evaluate how their organization functions. Rather than focusing solely on scaling existing processes, they must examine operations deeply, identifying gaps, inefficiencies, and opportunities for transformation. Many leaders fall into the trap of conducting surface-level evaluations, often relying on the perspectives of key decision-makers without digging into the core of the organization's processes.

However, deep operational analysis provides invaluable insights that can lead to substantial improvements and breakthroughs. The goal of driving operational excellence is to ensure that an organization's operations are driving the intended results in the most efficient and effective way possible.

Operational assessments, evaluation, analysis, and *audits* are terms that can be used to describe these functions. But the terminology is less important than the execution. My analytical nature, combined with diverse skill sets and intellect, has made my ability to analyze and assess second nature to me. As a change agent type of leader, I dive into operations to figure out what is working and not working. This has allowed me to solve problems, improve operations, and create growth for organizations. Even when conducting initial discovery calls with potential clients, I am often praised for the value I provide in just an initial thirty-minute call. I recall one such discovery with a small service company looking to grow. The CEO praised me and suggested paying me because the free initial consult was so valuable to them. Just think of the value that a thorough and complete evaluation of operations can bring.

THE IMPORTANCE OF ASKING THE RIGHT QUESTIONS AND DRIVING CHANGE

Asking the right questions is a leadership superpower and a key element of being a curious leader because it uncovers blind spots, fuels innovation, and drives meaningful change. A curious leader doesn't simply ask, "What went wrong?" Instead, they ask questions that provoke deeper understanding, like "What systemic factors contributed to this issue?" This shift from blame to discovery helps foster a culture of inquiry and continuous improvement and is necessary in creating a curious culture and a growth mindset that allow for failure. The quality of the questions leaders ask sets the foundation for better decision-making and operational excellence.

Effective questioning is about challenging assumptions and opening up new perspectives. Consider a business facing declining sales. Instead of asking, "Why aren't we hitting our numbers?" leaders could ask, "What market shifts are we not seeing?" or "How have customer preferences changed, and how can we adapt?" These questions help illuminate the root causes of problems and open pathways to innovative solutions.

Leaders must be willing to lift every stone—to dig deep and explore every aspect of their business operations without leaving any issue unexamined. This means refusing to accept surface-level answers and instead pushing for a deeper understanding of the root causes of challenges or opportunities. Lifting every stone requires curiosity and a commitment to uncovering what's beneath the obvious. It's about asking follow-up questions, challenging assumptions, and diving into the details that others might overlook. Whether it's identifying inefficiencies in a process, uncovering hidden team dynamics, or finding untapped potential in the market, leaders who lift every stone leave no area unexplored, ensuring that they have a full understanding before making decisions. This thorough approach reveals critical insights and fosters a culture of diligence, transparency, and accountability, where every team member is encouraged to be inquisitive and seek deeper knowledge.

Leaders must also ask questions that clarify organizational priorities. For example, "Are we focused on the initiatives that provide the highest returns?" can realign teams to the strategic goals that matter most. Asking questions like "What processes add the most value, and which can be eliminated without compromising quality?" can uncover inefficiencies and lead to streamlined operations.

I know this concept seems very simple and straightforward. But a key to asking the right question is getting to the heart of what you want to know. Often, we dance around what we are truly after, asking related but unimportant questions.

Take, for example, what happened when my wife and I were looking to tap into holiday deals for our cell phones—a process that would also require us to upgrade our plans. The cost to upgrade to the required plan was nominal—it was basically the same price. However, there were stated differences in the plans. For example, our current plan had international travel pass days as credits. Since my wife and I usually do some kind of trip outside the US each year, this was important to us. When she asked the cellular provider if we would lose travel pass days if we upgraded, customer service told her yes. When I looked into it, I discovered something different. The new plan would give us automatic coverage in two hundred and ten countries. When she asked if the new plan had travel pass days, my wife was given both an incorrect and a correct answer. The answer that the upgrade would not have them was correct. But the incorrect part was that the answer failed to address the context of the intended question. We were going to lose those travel pass days because they would no longer be required. The question for customer service was honest. The response was honest, even if it missed some nuance. An open-ended question about what happens under the new plan would have generated a more accurate response rather than granular

> **But a key to asking the right question is getting to the heart of what you want to know.**

information on the specific feature. This simple conversation showcases that it is important to ask the right question that gets to the heart of what you really want to know. In this case it would be, "How does the new plan handle international travel?" That would have likely brought up that we were going to be covered fully in the new plan.

Throughout my career, I have stepped into many situations and solved problems just by asking the right question(s). To solve problems, you have to first ensure that you are properly indicating what the problem is. Asking the right questions is critical to ascertaining that information. Once the problem is pinpointed, being curious, inquisitive, and asking questions is necessary if you want to find the solutions.

Beyond problem-solving, asking future-oriented questions is essential for driving innovation. A leader might ask, "What emerging technologies could help us leapfrog competitors?" or "How can we better serve our customers in ways they haven't anticipated yet?" These forward-looking questions encourage teams to think creatively, positioning the organization for long-term growth.

The right questions create a culture of curiosity and continuous improvement. It's not about solving just today's problems. It's about setting the stage for future success. Ultimately, leaders who master the art of asking powerful questions are better equipped to navigate complexity and foster a dynamic, innovative organization.

Let's be very clear. This is not about change for the sake of change. This is about removing the blind spots for continual innovation, growth, and change. Seeking and evaluating is not about judgment but about pivoting in the right direction. Again, learn from the greatest soccer coach of all time,

Ted Lasso, who said, "Be curious, not judgmental." Although this statement involves people and applies to culture, it is also important to remember when evaluating operations.

When I worked for an organization that hired me to bring about tremendous change, I actually had to stop using the word *change*. The staff were getting incredibly defensive because they interpreted *change* as an accusation that they were doing something wrong. Developing a curious culture has to allow for adaptability and pivoting. But part of a curious culture is also creating that psychological safety. In fact, the staff were not doing anything *wrong* at all. The staff were doing exactly what previous managers and leadership had asked them to do. But those actions were not working. Therefore, major changes had to be implemented across the organization, and many were brought on very quickly. To address the concerns, I pivoted to using the term *redirection*. This made a huge difference in morale as we navigated these changes. The intentions were to ask curious questions and make changes—not issue judgments.

Change is tough—I've seen it firsthand. It has to be led thoughtfully, not just pushed onto people. I've worked with teams where change happened so fast and hard that it caused more problems than it solved, leaving people overwhelmed and resistant. I've also walked into situations where immediate action was critical; making big changes quickly was the only way to stop the bleeding and give the organization a fighting chance to turn around.

Each situation is unique, and it takes a careful, empathetic approach to know when to push forward and when to slow down. That balance is essential, and it comes only from genuinely understanding what the organization and its people need at that moment.

TOOLS AND TECHNIQUES FOR EFFECTIVE QUESTIONING

Successfully questioning a business's operations requires structured tools and techniques. It's not enough to simply ask questions; leaders must use the right frameworks to dig deeper and generate actionable insights. Below are some essential tools that can help leaders investigate their business operations in a meaningful way:

- **The five *whys* technique:** This simple but powerful tool helps get to the root cause of a problem. By asking "Why?" repeatedly (typically five times), leaders can go beyond superficial answers and uncover underlying issues. For example, if a project is delayed, the first answer might be, "We didn't have enough resources." But by continuing to use the word *why*, the leader might discover the true cause to be poor project planning, unclear objectives, or ineffective communication.
- **SMART questions:** Just like setting SMART goals (Specific, Measurable, Achievable, Relevant, and Time-Bound), asking SMART questions ensures that inquiries are focused and actionable. Instead of vague questions like "How can we improve customer service?" a SMART question would be "What specific changes can we make to our customer service processes in the next quarter that will increase customer satisfaction by 15 percent?"
- **SWOT analysis:** A classic but highly effective tool for questioning business operations, SWOT analysis (Strengths, Weaknesses, Opportunities, Threats) helps leaders evaluate both internal and external factors. For instance, leaders can take a balanced approach by asking, "What are our current strengths, and how can we leverage them to seize new opportunities?"

or "What external threats are we not addressing that could harm our long-term success?" However, it is vitally important that a SWOT analysis is not superficial. What I mean by that is that it can't be the same individuals discussing their thoughts but needs to go deeper.
- **Benchmarking:** Benchmarking involves comparing an organization's processes and performance metrics against industry best practices or competitors. This helps leaders identify gaps and opportunities for improvement. Key questions could include "Where are we underperforming compared to industry standards?" and "What practices from top competitors could we adopt to improve our efficiency?"
- **Brainstorming and collaboration:** Encouraging open-ended questioning through group collaboration can lead to more innovative solutions. Techniques like Edward de Bono's Six Thinking Hats, which encourages team members to explore a problem from multiple perspectives (emotional, logical, creative), help generate fresh insights.
- **Data-driven inquiry:** Data analytics tools enable leaders to ask more precise, evidence-based questions. For example, using sales data, leaders can ask, "What are the trends in customer buying behavior over the past year?" or "Which products are performing below average, and why?" Data-backed questions lead to more informed decisions and allow for deeper analysis of operational performance.
- **Creating a safe space for questions:** An organization that fosters curiosity encourages employees to ask questions without fear of repercussions. Regular review meetings where open-ended questions are encouraged help surface issues that might otherwise remain hidden.

By creating an environment where questioning is celebrated, leaders enable deeper analysis and discovery.

SEEKING EXTERNAL HELP

One of the greatest challenges leaders face when evaluating their organizations is the presence of biases, traditions, habits, and blind spots that may cloud their judgment. These ingrained tendencies can prevent leaders and their teams from seeing inefficiencies or hidden opportunities in their people, processes, and platforms. When you rely solely on your own thoughts or those of your team, there's a risk that personal biases, long-standing traditions, or comfort with the status quo may hinder objective analysis. This is when seeking external help can be invaluable.

By bringing in a neutral third party, such as a consultant, you gain access to a fresh set of eyes—someone who can view the organization from an unbiased outsider's perspective. Consultants have no preconceived notions about the internal politics, traditions, or assumptions that may influence internal decision-making. Their ability to ask probing, uncomfortable questions allows them to dig deeper and go beyond surface-level assessments. With their specialized tools, frameworks, and methodologies, consultants can conduct thorough evaluations, identify hidden inefficiencies, and provide insights that may otherwise go unnoticed.

Furthermore, consultants can challenge assumptions and help an organization break free from the inertia that often comes with long-standing practices. Since they don't have the same blind spots, they can offer objective analysis and actionable recommendations that drive meaningful change. For leaders seeking to transform their business operations and make informed decisions, relying on an external consultant can be a crucial step in achieving a more comprehensive and effective evaluation.

By combining these tools and techniques, leaders create a culture where curiosity thrives and operational excellence is continuously pursued. Leaders who ask the right questions—and empower their teams to do the same—unlock new insights that drive growth, innovation, and competitive advantage.

ANALYZING AND IMPROVING BUSINESS PROCESSES

To maintain long-term success, businesses must continuously evaluate and refine their processes. It's not just about getting results—it's about getting those results in the most efficient and effective way possible. This means identifying gaps, redundancies, inefficiencies, and anything else that might hinder optimal performance. Process improvement is about ensuring that your organization's operations are not just functioning but functioning at their best. No systems should be set up and completely ignored. Spot-checks, quality control, and even reevaluation of the effectiveness and efficiency of the processes are needed.

Even basic functions, such as accounting, invoicing, and money collection, need constant review of processes and procedures. EV auto manufacturer Fisker seemed to be facing imminent demise in a bankruptcy without a safety blanket, or at least the serious issues started coming to light in late 2023. Although many challenges led to its demise, its accounting and internal processes are a case study that showcases just how important basic business functions are. Once the company filed for bankruptcy, more information came out about the complete lack of processes and the impact it had on the company's revenue and cash flow. It is my understanding that much of this came out during Nissan's due diligence as it was considering acquiring the company. Discoveries highlighted that, in some cases, Fisker had been shipping vehicles without accepting payments. In other cases, it failed to cash checks and record payments. The stories that arose paint a picture of a completely disorganized system in which employees were constantly scrambling to figure out the facts, tracking down money, and figuring out what was up from down. Reports indicated that information was not properly provided to various departments and parties involved, and that led to them taking action before it was appropriate.

This report paints a picture of complete and utter chaos. And think about this. This is not a software subscription, a steak dinner, or a pair of shoes. These are $30,000, $60,000, and even $80,000 vehicles that were shipped without accepting or properly recording payment.

Leaders who ask the right questions—and empower their teams to do the same—unlock new insights that drive growth, innovation, and competitive advantage.

Obviously, Fisker's case is extreme, but this happens in everyday businesses. Systems break down or are never created in the first place far more often than most would like to admit. It often happens when a founder, owner, or CEO wants to control all communication and interaction with customers and clients. This gets even worse when they think they are diligent enough to handle the accounting side of those interactions.

Here is what happens: Things get missed. Let's say there's a startup with tight cash flow and a slowly growing revenue. Then someone realizes that an invoice has been on the books for a year now and was never sent to the client. Now, many things are going on in this scenario. In this situation, the CEO is prematurely entering invoices before they have been 100 percent confirmed. Keeping this invoice on the books is aspirational, but it has never been handed off to someone to manage. When accountants are closing out the following year's books, it gets flagged again. But now, so much time has passed that no one remembers what happened, and the company is stuck trying to submit an invoice that is over a year old.

I have another example of a case where there was a lot of confusion around processes and a desire to control the process. I was involved in overseeing a merger between two service agencies. One of those agencies was actually a third-party contractor of the other and decided to merge. Now, mergers will never go 100 percent as planned. But the key is to be curious and creative in solving the problems. In this situation, the acquired company wanted to dictate how its clients were contacted, invoiced, etc. Here's the problem: The partner dictating the process was constantly upset with his involvement in it. He failed to see that he was the hurdle he wanted to fix. He did not really want to be involved, but he kept requiring his involvement. So the process was always changing. At one point, we were more than a month late in invoicing monthly retainers. I was following up with the partner on a regular basis but was being ignored. Finally, he blew up and demanded to know why we hadn't invoiced the clients. The answer was that he'd said he wanted to review a summary before we invoiced, but he had not reviewed what was submitted.

It is important to set up processes and procedures that are focused on getting the intended results. Partners, owners, CEOs, and founders have to allow the professionals to dictate a system that will work, then trust it. It is important to have people involved in the process only when necessary.

I once worked with a marketing service firm that experienced significant delays in receivables, often extending beyond the normal industry standards of thirty to sixty days for small-to-medium-sized businesses. While large enterprises may take sixty to ninety days, this was unusual for the firm's typical client base. I kept explaining that one of the problems was that this firm did not accept digital payments other than credit cards. Of course, credit cards have their own issues, especially when you are talking about larger consulting fees. I kept trying to convince this marketing firm to put out its banking information or adopt an AP/AR system that allowed for more seamless payments. But the leaders were skeptical. Then COVID hit, and the situation got worse. We all remember the many processes and supply chain issues, including delayed mail delivery, that occurred. This situation finally got the leaders to adopt more of a digital process for their receivables, and they saw an immediate and significant reduction in days out.

Evaluating processes means going beyond assumptions and challenging the way things have always been done. Leaders must be willing to dive deep and ask, "Are we achieving the desired outcomes with the least amount of waste, time, and resources? Are there steps in our processes that are outdated, unnecessary, or bottlenecking progress?" By committing to a regular review of business operations, organizations can ensure that they are continually optimizing and evolving to meet new challenges.

To improve processes effectively, leaders should follow a systematic approach that involves:

1. **Identifying:** Start by identifying areas in the organization where processes might be underperforming. This can include looking at metrics like time, cost, output, and quality. It's important to pinpoint where inefficiencies or bottlenecks are happening so you can take action.

2. **Collecting:** Gather data and feedback from those closest to the process—often, this means frontline employees. They can provide invaluable insights into where issues lie or what parts of the process create the most frustration or inefficiency. Collect both qualitative and quantitative data to get a full picture.

3. **Assessing:** Once you have the data, assess it to understand what's working and what's not. This step requires a critical eye to spot gaps, redundancies, or unnecessary complexity. This is where curiosity plays a big role: Leaders must be willing to question existing methods and dig deeper to uncover the real issues.

4. **Acting:** Finally, implement changes based on the findings. This could mean streamlining processes, introducing new technology, or eliminating unnecessary steps. After making changes, continuously monitor the results and be open to making further adjustments as needed. Improvement is an ongoing process.

It's also important to review technology when evaluating processes. Technology and software are crucial for streamlining and optimizing business processes. However, leaders must be strategic in selecting tools that enhance efficiency rather than piling on band-aid solutions or nice-to-have software that doesn't integrate well with existing systems. When too many disconnected platforms are in use, they can lead to silos, inefficiencies, and communication breakdowns. Instead, businesses should prioritize comprehensive, integrated solutions—such as enterprise resource planning (ERP) systems—that work together seamlessly. Today's software is designed to connect with other systems. Zapier is a great example of a tool that allows businesses to easily integrate software solutions that do not have native integrations. Strategies must ensure that the technology supports the overall process improvement goals, driving both efficiency and cohesion across the organization.

When I started working with one particular business, I walked into my office to find a spiderweb diagram of software solutions. I had a call with my predecessor, who walked me through the board. As discussed earlier, identifying processes is the first step in the analysis phase. In this situation, the collective group of software was the process that needed to be reviewed.

Evaluating processes means going beyond assumptions and challenging the way things have always been done.

The spiderweb of software solutions was, for the most part, completely disjointed. When a department had a software solution they believed would help their operations, they would get it. There was no internal discussion about whether it worked with current systems and software. There was just one vetting question: "Do we want it?" That was it. This laissez-faire attitude toward software solutions—with no one monitoring the overall software solution strategy—created a nightmare.

I had to unravel these systems and even require staff to cancel some subscriptions and research additional solutions that were in the current systems or could natively integrate. The problem with too many solutions that do not natively integrate is that they require additional software that connects the two. Sometimes, even two different integrating solutions are needed. Each piece of software and connection involved creates an opportunity for the connection and process to break down. It takes an enormous amount of work to ensure that everything is working, and it takes even more work when the system collapses. This is why there needs to be a strategy behind your software solutions. When you have a strategy, the solutions create efficacy in the business, and they help more than hurt.

SYSTEMS AND METHODOLOGIES FOR PROCESS IMPROVEMENT

Once you've laid the groundwork for improving processes, proven methodologies can help refine your approach. Two of the most effective frameworks are lean principles and Six Sigma.

Lean principles focus on eliminating waste and improving efficiency by streamlining processes that do not add value from the customer's perspective. Leaders using lean should ask, "What steps in this process can be removed without impacting quality or customer satisfaction?" The goal is to maximize value while minimizing unnecessary steps, resources, or time. A hallmark of my career has been launching efficient and effective internal operations with the mindset of increasing staff satisfaction and reducing the work needed to manage the administrative functions.

Six Sigma uses statistical tools to minimize variation and defects in processes, driving high-quality outcomes. Leaders can ask, "How can we reduce errors in this process by 20 percent in the next quarter?" This framework focuses on consistency and precision, ensuring that the processes deliver results with minimal defects or inefficiencies.

By combining these two methodologies, organizations can use Lean Six Sigma to balance both speed and quality. Lean focuses on reducing waste and improving speed, while Six Sigma creates accurate and high-quality processes. Together, they create an approach that is both efficient and effective.

I have studied these types of systems and even frameworks like the Entrepreneurial Operating System (EOS). But more important than any one system is the mindset behind it. The desire to be curious and analyze your operations to find efficacy is more important than choosing a particular framework or system. When I first read *Traction: Get a Grip on Your Business* and learned about EOS, it was clear that I had been implementing the components and intentions of their system, just without the name.

CASE STUDY: THE MICROMANAGING MANAGER

I once worked with a manager whom I was convinced was micromanaging her staff, though she didn't recognize this behavior in herself. The manager was open to feedback, so I spoke to her staff to get a clearer picture. Interestingly, when I asked the team if they felt micromanaged, their initial response was unequivocally no. But I didn't stop there—my curiosity and questions went deeper. I asked more probing questions, like "Is it more important to get the results or to follow her process?" They answered that it was more important to follow her process.

I followed up with "If you didn't follow her process but got the result in fewer steps, would you be in trouble?" The answer was unequivocally yes. This illuminated that while the staff didn't explicitly feel micromanaged, they were held back by rigid processes that limited their ability to innovate and find more efficient ways to achieve the desired results.

This situation demonstrates the power of curiosity in process evaluation. By asking the right questions and observing the dynamics within the team, I was able to identify an inefficiency in the management style that was impeding process improvement. Micromanagement is the enemy of curiosity and progress—it stifles initiative, creativity, and the opportunity to find better ways to get things done.

Leaders must remain open to evaluating both their processes and their own behaviors. By encouraging staff to explore alternative methods and focus on outcomes rather than rigid processes, they can foster a culture of continuous improvement and curiosity. This mindset improves efficiency and empowers employees to take ownership of their work and find better, faster ways to achieve success.

FOUR OPERATIONAL AREAS TO ASSESS FOR EXCELLENCE IN YOUR ORGANIZATION

In any successful organization, certain operational areas must be regularly assessed to ensure that the business is operating efficiently, adapting to change, and driving growth. By focusing on these key areas, leaders can create a robust infrastructure that promotes long-term success and sustainability. Here are four critical operational areas to assess:

Decision-Making Framework

A clear and effective decision-making framework is the backbone of aligning an organization's actions with its identity, values, and long-term goals. It's more than just a set of processes. It's a way to guarantee that decisions consistently reflect the organization's purpose and mission. I've seen firsthand what happens when this framework is missing. During one project involving a merger, I wasn't given the proper authority to execute decisions, and the person who was in control wasn't driving the process. It created unnecessary roadblocks and delays, which directly impacted cash flow, client satisfaction, resource management, and even team morale. Without clarity in decision-making, the entire system becomes stuck, and the repercussions ripple outward.

At its core, a strong decision-making framework brings alignment among leadership and ensures that everyone shares a common vision for where the organization is going and how to get there. One of the biggest pitfalls I've seen, particularly in startups, small businesses, and nonprofits, is a lack of proper delegation when it comes to decision-making. It's not uncommon to see founders or leaders holding on to every decision, slowing progress, and inadvertently stifling the team's ability to act. Without a clear framework, decision-making becomes chaotic, and the organization loses its direction.

This is why decision-making must be tied to an organization's core identity. It requires clear and well-defined values, a vision that inspires, and a mission that grounds every choice. It also demands a consistent process for gathering input, analyzing data, and ensuring that decisions align with those principles. A framework like this supports daily operations and serves as a guide for larger strategic initiatives, creating clarity and consistency that lead to better results.

Alignment is not just about delegation, of course. It's also about aligning leadership and management in the overall process. Do the CEO and COO view change, innovation, culture, etc., the same? If not, serious issues can occur, including a lack of results and even backtracking on successes that have been achieved. Without proper alignment, animosities can set in, which will undoubtedly create setbacks. If one person is making and executing on decisions that the other does not agree with, there's a risk of actions being undone. It is not just about the relationship between the two executives. It also transfers down to the rest of the staff.

I saw this firsthand when I was COO for an organization. We had made some great changes, but there was a point where the alignment fell apart. In all honesty, some of this was my fault for not managing up as well as I should have. It doesn't matter how many successes an organization has. If the executives are not aligned, those successes will be short-lived.

IKEA is an excellent example of a company that has mastered this alignment. Its identity is rooted in offering affordable, well-designed, and functional home furnishings while promoting sustainability and a positive societal impact. During my younger years, I had furnished nearly my entire apartment with IKEA products, so I'd seen firsthand the brilliance of its model. The furniture was stylish, practical, and affordable—a trifecta that resonated deeply with me as a broke young professional who was willing to spend a few hours assembling a bookshelf rather than pay for a more expensive alternative.

What makes IKEA stand out is how deeply its values influence its leadership's decision-making. For example, its commitment to sustainability isn't just a marketing point. That commitment is embedded in the company's operations. By 2030, IKEA plans to use only renewable or recycled materials in its products and has already invested heavily in renewable energy, owning more wind turbines than stores. Even its flat-pack furniture is a reflection of those values, minimizing packaging and transportation costs while reducing the company's environmental footprint.

IKEA's ability to align its decisions with its core identity has also fueled innovation. Take its augmented reality app, IKEA Place, which allows customers to visualize how furniture will look in their homes before making a purchase. This wasn't just a tech gimmick—it was a thoughtful decision to enhance the customer experience while staying true to IKEA's mission of accessibility and functionality.

The results of this alignment are undeniable. IKEA's commitment to its identity has built global brand loyalty, driven financial success, and positioned the company as a leader in sustainability. Customers trust IKEA because its decisions consistently reflect its values. But this doesn't happen by chance—it's the result of a strong decision-making framework that makes sure every choice supports the company's purpose.

Reflecting on IKEA's story, I'm reminded of how easy it is for organizations to lose sight of the principles that got them to where they are. Success can sometimes lead to complacency or, worse, a departure from the values that drove that success in the first place.

As a curious leader, it's your responsibility to challenge the status quo while staying true to your organization's identity. Curiosity doesn't mean abandoning your core—it means ensuring that every decision you make builds on it. That's what drives sustainable success.

Adaptability (People's Capacity for Change) and Culture

An organization's ability to adapt doesn't just lie in its systems or processes—it depends on the people who make it run. Organizations are made up of individuals, each bringing their habits, fears, traditions, and biases into the mix. True adaptability emerges from the willingness of people—leaders and employees alike—to embrace change, learn new skills, and shift mindsets. It's a deeply human quality that drives an organization's ability to pivot in uncertain times and seize opportunities as they arise.

In my work, I've seen firsthand how adaptability—or the lack of it—can make or break an organization. I've worked with teams that struggled because employees resisted learning a new technology or process and with leaders who refused to adjust their approach based on feedback. These situations created bottlenecks, stifled innovation, and, in some cases, caused the organization to lose its competitive edge. It's not enough for leadership to be adaptable; the entire organization needs to be on board. From senior executives to the most junior staff, everyone must play a role in fostering flexibility and a mindset of continuous growth.

Adaptability matters because it allows organizations to pivot when the unexpected happens. Think back to the massive global shift to remote work. Companies with adaptable employees transitioned smoothly, maintaining productivity and morale. But those with rigid cultures, where change was met with resistance, struggled to stay cohesive. The ability to adapt quickly wasn't about having the best tools or technology—it was about the mindset of the people involved.

One of the best examples of adaptability on a grand scale is Netflix. I'll admit that I still smile when I think about those red DVD envelopes that used to show up in the mail. The whole operation worked so seamlessly. But what's even more remarkable is how Netflix didn't just rest on its initial success. The company pivoted from DVD rentals to streaming, then pivoted again to become a global powerhouse in original content production. That kind of transformation doesn't happen by accident. It takes leadership with a vision for change—middle managers who can translate that vision into action and employees who are willing to embrace a new way of doing things.

Netflix's adaptability starts at the top. Reed Hastings, the company's CEO, recognized early on that physical media was on its way out. He led the company through a monumental shift to streaming, taking risks that many would have avoided. But leadership alone wasn't enough. The entire organization had to adapt. Employees had to embrace a culture of freedom and responsibility, where they were empowered to make decisions and experiment. This culture fostered a mindset of ownership and curiosity, enabling the company to navigate shifts in viewer preferences and market demands with agility.

I've always believed that communication is the most critical tool for leading change, and Netflix exemplifies this. Internally, the company is transparent about its goals and strategies, ensuring that everyone understands the why behind each decision. Externally, Netflix communicates its vision clearly, building trust with stakeholders and customers alike. When

I've led organizations through significant changes, I've leaned heavily on overcommunication. I've made sure to explain not just what was happening but why it mattered, what outcomes we expected, and what role each person would play. That level of clarity makes all the difference in bringing people along for the journey.

The results of Netflix's adaptability speak for themselves. The company transitioned from a small DVD rental service into the global leader in streaming—a brand synonymous with innovation and entertainment. Its success wasn't just about embracing new technology. It was about fostering a mindset at every level of the organization that welcomed change and saw it as an opportunity rather than a threat.

Organizations must cultivate adaptability intentionally. It's not about reacting to change when it comes—it's about preparing for it, embracing it, and using it as a springboard for growth. When leaders foster adaptability within their teams, they create organizations that are resilient, innovative, and ready to thrive no matter what challenges lie ahead. Netflix's story isn't more than a case study in adaptability. It's a testament to what's possible when every person in an organization is committed to change.

Adaptability and the reinforcement of that in the organization is absolutely part of the culture. The overall culture needs to be regularly assessed and evaluated for adaptability and beyond to ensure that the culture being built is the intended culture. Do you have the mechanisms in place to evaluate the culture? This is the reason that I am developing an assessment on curious leadership as well as curious culture. Everything is related in these topics where the mindset, the culture, and operations are all intertwined and no element should be immune from questioning and evaluation.

Let's make sure we are not ignoring the elephant in the room. Change is hard! I talked about this earlier in the book, but it is important to reinforce it here as well. I have worked with many associations on personal and professional levels. An association's volunteers, directors, and staff alike are dedicated individuals. But here's the problem: They tend to like the association for what it is, not what it can be. They cling to the norms and traditions, sometimes even while driving the truck (the association) right off a cliff (irrelevance, decline, and even closure). Curiosity is about setting new paths, challenging the status quo, and bringing everyone along for these changes. Everyone involved in the process has to have the capacity for change.

Operational Strength

Operational strength is the backbone of any organization that strives for sustainable growth and excellence. It's about refining and optimizing internal processes so that resources are allocated effectively. It's also about building resilience against disruptions. For me, operational strength has always meant one thing: taking a step back, scrutinizing every detail of how things run, and asking, "Is this the best way to do it?" It's about creating systems that don't just function but thrive, allowing the organization to achieve its goals with efficiency and effectiveness. This is the essence of operational excellence.

In my work with organizations, I've often found that operational weaknesses aren't caused by a lack of effort but by a lack of clarity. Without a structured approach to evaluating processes, resource allocation, and risk management, a company ends up guessing—sometimes chasing initiatives that don't align with its goals or failing to address inefficiencies that hold it back. I've seen this firsthand, where organizations pour time and money into flashy solutions while overlooking fundamental gaps in their operations. That's why an operational assessment is so critical: It brings clarity and ensures that resources are applied where they'll have the greatest impact.

Amazon is the quintessential example of operational strength in action. From its humble beginnings as an online bookstore to its current status as a global juggernaut, Amazon's success is rooted in its relentless commitment to operational excellence. I still marvel at how seamlessly its systems work—from the moment you place an order to when that package arrives at your doorstep, sometimes within hours. It's not magic. It's the result of finely tuned processes, advanced technology, and an unwavering focus on improvement.

Amazon's supply chain is a masterclass in standardization and optimization. Every fulfillment center operates like clockwork, with meticulously documented processes resulting in consistency and minimal errors. I've often thought about how Amazon's ability to get millions of packages out the door each day mirrors the precision of a finely tuned orchestra—all the pieces working together seamlessly to deliver a flawless performance.

But it's not just about efficiency. It's also about foresight and adaptability. Amazon's leadership, particularly Jeff Bezos, had the vision to invest in automation and advanced analytics long before they became industry norms. The company's warehouses, powered by robotic systems and machine learning, aren't just efficient—they're scalable and capable of handling demand surges like those seen during the holiday season or even the pandemic. This adaptability allowed Amazon to meet unprecedented challenges without skipping a beat.

One of my favorite stories about Amazon's operational strength is the birth of Amazon Web Services (AWS). Originally developed to address internal needs for data storage and computing power, AWS grew out of a simple question: "Could this help others?" That question led to the creation of a platform that revolutionized cloud computing, enabling startups and developers to build and scale software in ways that were previously unimaginable. It's a perfect example of how operational innovation can spark entirely new business opportunities.

Amazon's operational maturity doesn't just deliver results—it builds trust. Customers know they can rely on Amazon for fast, reliable service, and that trust translates into loyalty. It's a reminder that operational strength isn't just about what happens behind the scenes. It's about the impact those operations have on the people you serve.

For leaders, the lesson here is clear: Operational strength doesn't happen by accident. It requires a commitment to questioning processes, optimizing resources, and building systems that can adapt and scale. It's about finding the balance between efficiency and innovation, ensuring your organization is prepared not just for today but for whatever challenges and opportunities lie ahead. Amazon has set the bar high, but its success is a testament to what's possible when operational strength is at the heart of everything you do.

Operational Efficiency

At the heart of any thriving organization lies operational efficiency—using resources like time, money, and talent in the most effective way possible to achieve results. For businesses, especially smaller ones with fewer resources, efficiency is not just a metric—it's a survival strategy. And while operational strength provides the foundation for growth, operational efficiency ensures that you get there with minimal waste and maximum impact. Equally important is compliance—adhering to legal and industry standards to protect the organization from risks while maintaining trust among stakeholders.

I've worked with startups and small businesses that were filled with potential yet were stuck in inefficiency. One particular startup comes to mind. The founder was deeply passionate about the organization's vision but was drowning in operational chaos. Payroll processes were manual, scheduling was a nightmare, and administrative tasks consumed most of the team's energy. The lack of streamlined systems slowed the startup down and kept it from focusing on growth and innovation.

The first step was auditing its processes and asking tough questions: "Why are we doing it this way? Is this necessary? What could make this simpler?" By mapping workflows, eliminating redundancies, and automating repetitive tasks, we freed up significant time and resources. For example, by introducing software for payroll and invoicing, the team eliminated hours of manual work every week, allowing them to focus on revenue-generating activities instead.

Another key shift was empowering the founder to step out of the weeds. Leaders should be strategizing and driving growth, not bogged down in daily operations. By implementing clear accountability systems and delegating operational tasks to capable team members, we created a structure that let the founder concentrate on scaling the business. This wasn't just about freeing their time—it was about enabling them to do what they do best: lead.

Operational efficiency also requires a commitment to quality control and compliance. Standardized processes ensured that nothing fell through the cracks, from meeting regulatory requirements to delivering a consistent customer experience. Regular audits and checkpoints caught small errors before they became costly issues. This protected the company from risk and built trust with customers and investors alike.

Technology played a critical role in making the business scalable. From project management tools to customer relationship management systems, every piece of software was chosen with one goal in mind: to simplify and optimize operations. This use of technology didn't just save time—it allowed the company to expand without the growing pains associated with scaling inefficient processes.

The results were transformative. The business reduced administrative tasks by nearly 40 percent, enabling the team to focus on clients and growth. No longer burdened by operational minutiae, the founder reported a renewed sense of clarity and purpose. They had the bandwidth to think strategically, pursue partnerships, and innovate in their industry.

Operational efficiency isn't just about cutting costs or doing things faster. It's about creating an ecosystem where every resource is directed toward meaningful outcomes. It's about empowering teams to perform at their best while giving leaders the space to lead. When done right, operational efficiency drives profitability and growth as well as creates peace of mind—allowing leaders to focus on the future while knowing the foundation of their business is strong and sustainable.

INTERCONNECTED FOUNDATIONS OF OPERATIONAL EXCELLENCE

Running a fully operational, mature business means building an environment where decision-making alignment, adaptability, operational maturity, efficiency, and compliance coexist and reinforce one another. Each element is critical to the whole, and they all work in tandem to support a resilient, innovative, and forward-thinking organization.

A strong decision-making framework anchors the business, aligning actions with strategic goals and values, which is essential for guiding every operational choice. However, even the most aligned decisions lack power if the organization isn't adaptable and prepared to respond to market shifts, emerging challenges, or new opportunities. Adaptability supports operational maturity, enabling the organization to scale and evolve without sacrificing quality or consistency. Mature operations provide the backbone needed to structure complex activities and manage resources efficiently, yet operational efficiency and compliance ensure that these resources are used wisely, upholding standards and minimizing risks.

None of these areas can stand alone; a well-functioning, operationally mature business requires a balance across all four categories. An adaptable business with misaligned decisions will drift off course, while operational efficiency without adaptability leads to rigidity. For true innovation, growth, and change, these elements must be interwoven, creating a dynamic structure that supports sustainable success and resilience.

CHAPTER 7
DESIRED BUSINESS OUTCOMES OF CURIOSITY-DRIVEN LEADERSHIP

"Curiosity is the engine of achievement."
—Ken Robinson

Given today's fast pace of change in the business world, cultivating and creating your organization's curiosity competence can be a competitive engine for long-term success. After all, curiosity cultivates change, fueling growth, and innovation. Curiosity-driven leadership is not merely about creating a workplace where inquiry and exploration are encouraged. It is about translating that curiosity into valuable, actionable outcomes for the organization. By recognizing the power of curiosity and actively cultivating it for their teams, curious leaders help generate innovation, adaptability, and continuous improvement, which continually moves the company forward.

In this chapter, we look at the various results an organization can achieve through curiosity-driven leadership. We examine the quantitative metrics and key qualitative outcomes that reveal whether an organization benefits from having curiosity as a competence. We look at the kinds of people transformations (engaged employees) that a company can enact through curiosity and product transformations (successful implementation and use of groundbreaking technologies) to create new-to-the-world results.

DEFINING SUCCESS THROUGH THE LENS OF CURIOSITY

The success that curiosity can drive in an organization goes far beyond traditional metrics. It's not just about numbers on a spreadsheet or quarterly reports. It's about fostering a deeper sense of growth, creativity, and connection in the organization. The real power of curiosity became clear to me when I started noticing how much richer the conversations, ideas, and solutions became in organizations that embraced it fully.

One of the most exciting transformations I've seen is a surge in innovation that was created by prioritizing curiosity as is seen in famous examples provided throughout this book. When people feel empowered to ask questions and explore new ideas, creativity blossoms. I've seen this firsthand in teams where questioning the status quo led to groundbreaking solutions—ideas that would never have surfaced if everyone had just followed the old playbook. These moments of innovation aren't just exciting. They propel the organization forward, allowing it to leap ahead in ways that no one thought possible.

But curiosity doesn't just drive innovation. It transforms the culture. I've watched engagement and job satisfaction soar when employees are encouraged to connect their work with their passions. There's something incredibly fulfilling about seeing someone light up because they've been given the space to explore a part of their expertise or interest that wasn't previously tapped. I think about a team member who once told me, "I never thought I'd get to use my interest in environmental science in this role, but here I am, contributing to sustainability initiatives." That spark of curiosity led to not just personal satisfaction but a tangible impact on the organization.

Curiosity drives leaders and executives to think bigger, including about the impossible. Although Elon Musk may be considered controversial by some, there's no doubt that he is a visionary. The views he has on living on Mars are things that drive Hollywood blockbusters, but he believes it a reality. More than just mindset, leaders who adopt curiosity constantly drive their organizations to improve and create efficiencies. They are not comfortable or complacent with the way things are but are constantly seeking ways to improve.

Curiosity doesn't just drive innovation. It transforms the culture.

Curiosity also creates a culture that can adapt and thrive amid change. People become more agile and open to shifting course when they are encouraged to ask, "What if?" or "Why not?" I've seen teams respond to unexpected market changes with confidence because they weren't locked into rigid ways of thinking. Instead, they embraced the change as an opportunity to explore new paths. This agility isn't just nice to have. It's essential in today's fast-moving business environment.

A curious culture also fosters learning and development at every level. I've worked in organizations where employees were constantly encouraged to deepen their understanding—not just of the business but of themselves. Curiosity becomes a catalyst for growth, pushing people to expand their skills and perspectives. It's amazing how much progress can happen when people feel safe and supported to explore new areas of learning.

And perhaps most importantly, curiosity strengthens collaboration. In environments where questions are welcomed and ideas are valued, people naturally work better together. They share knowledge more freely, tackle challenges with less defensiveness, and approach their work as a collective effort rather than a solo endeavor. This collaborative energy is contagious and often results in solutions that are greater than the sum of their parts.

Curiosity also builds resilience. Organizations that prioritize curiosity create a workforce that's comfortable with trying new things, failing, and learning from the process. This resourcefulness becomes the foundation for weathering challenges, whether they're internal struggles or external disruptions. I've seen organizations thrive during tough times because their people were empowered to think creatively and adapt rather than retreat into old patterns.

When we measure the impact of curiosity, we're measuring something far more enduring than short-term profits. Curiosity drives meaningful, lasting success by weaving values of learning, creativity, and renewal into the very fabric of the organization. It's not just about where you're going—it's about how you get there. Curiosity ensures that the journey is as transformative as the destination.

ENHANCED INNOVATION AND PROBLEM-SOLVING CAPABILITIES

Leadership based on an open desire to discover—curiosity-driven leadership—consistently raises an organization's capacity to innovate and solve problems. When leaders build an environment that tolerates and actively promotes questions and exploration, employees are encouraged to outgrow the boxes and methods of the past.

For one thing, in a work environment where curiosity is encouraged, the people doing the work are more likely to engage in thinking processes that can lead to creativity. If you ask employees to think about why things are the way they are and to figure out what would happen if things were changed, these questions will lead them to look at problems from new angles. Creativity often leads to someone seeing an opportunity that was first obscure but becomes obvious when they look in a certain way. We've seen numerous examples of how curiosity-provoking questions can lead to discussions about previously unnoticed resources and possibilities that can help resolve a problem more efficiently, even when significant hurdles block a complete resolution.

Curiosity drives all employees to think about what is wrong and how we can do it better. It drives people to not just accept the status quo but move beyond that to find a better way. If that is the normal state, what do you think happens when there is a problem? The entire team goes above and beyond to be creative in how they look at and define the problem as well as solve it!

Moreover, firms that cultivate curiosity tend to attract and keep people who are naturally curious and motivated to learn. These staff members are the most likely to push the boundaries of knowledge, make mistakes, learn from them, and drive new initiatives as a result.

A curiosity-driven environment fosters the sharing of ideas and insights, which means more collaboration. This further improves outcomes, as the collective brainstorming process often leads to richer answers and allows for the incorporation of diverse perspectives and expertise. Cross-pollination across departments and teams is more likely to create emergent, game-changing ideas than everyone working in the same bubble.

When these narrow stories embrace a broader culture of curiosity, they can also make organizations more resilient to the inevitable shifts that follow. Employees can learn to treat change and disruption not as a threat but as a chance to grow. They become more flexible and nimble in reacting to shifts in the market or technology.

In other words, an approach to leadership that fosters and encourages curiosity ultimately fosters innovation and future-proofs the organization through problem-solving. It also creates a culture that encourages continual improvement of everything—the product, service, business models, policies, processes, strategies, etc. In addition, it helps create a growth mindset, encouraging employees to stay the course and focus on continually growing their knowledge, skills, and wisdom.

To build curiosity-centered cultures, leaders must be examples by asking questions, seeking new information and perspectives, and being transparent about their lack of knowledge. Managers can create opportunities for learning and experimentation by sponsoring training programs or hackathons and fostering a learning culture where mistakes are treated as opportunities for growth rather than indications of failure.

Fostering a culture of curiosity is critical for the success of organizations in today's dynamic business environment. Organizations that encourage both individual and collective curiosity will be well-positioned to innovate, collaborate, be resilient, and enhance the effectiveness of their continuous improvement initiatives. Curious employees will be the ones blazing the trails of tomorrow in their organizations. It is, therefore, time for leaders to be curious and facilitate curiosity, driving the required learning, skill-building, and knowledge.

Curiosity brings personal growth and fulfillment to employees and organizations. Branching out into new directions can allow employees to escape the confines of familiar beliefs and behavior. This process can uplift their well-being by increasing job satisfaction, motivation, and engagement. Beyond that, curiosity can make employees more adaptive and resilient—qualities that are especially valuable during times of organizational change or uncertainty.

Because the business world is changing at an unprecedented rate, firms need to be open to adapting, innovating, and constantly improving if they want to stay ahead. Leaders who prioritize curiosity keep their teams thinking and encourage them to ask questions, challenge existing processes, and try new ways of doing things. So, let's be curious, create curious cultures, and let our organizations thrive for the long term.

We all need to keep learning and growing and asking, "What if?"

The next time you face a challenge or problem in your organization, rather than searching for quick wins or using the same old methods, engage your curiosity. Ask questions, explore viewpoints, experiment, and see where it takes you.

> **We all need to keep learning and growing and asking, "What if?"**

Curiosity can be an excellent tool that leadership can use to develop a culture where employees feel fulfilled professionally and in their personal lives. So, let's be curious, allow our emotions to drive our curiosity, and make it stretch past our limitations. Ask why, how, and what if, which are just the beginning. Let there be learning. Let there be joy from discovery and growth. There's no end when the mind is curious. Keep exploring. Keep evolving. And see where the journey takes you. The end of your day will never be the end of the day.

Cheers to a fulfilling life inspired by curiosity.

NASA LEADERS BREAKING FROM NORMS IN *THE MARTIAN*

Yes, I'm talking about the Matt Damon movie *The Martian*. You know—the movie where he gets left on Mars all by himself and has to find a way to, first of all, live and then, second, escape the planet and rejoin his team. During a horrible storm, Matt Damon is left on the planet and presumed to be dead. However, his team eventually discovers that is not the case, and the planning and decision-making to recover him get started.

The leaders and scientists on the ground have to find a way to rescue Matt Damon. As portrayed in *every* NASA-based movie, "NASA doesn't take chances; they double up on everything." (This is a quote from *Armageddon*.) NASA tests and retests and retests. Even commercial space outfits are continuously testing their capabilities and spacecrafts. Through this testing, we now have rocket ships that can take off and land themselves as opposed to splashing down in the Atlantic Ocean and leaving the astronauts hoping to be recovered before the capsule sinks.

But, in *The Martian*, their time is eventually up. Matt Damon's character is running out of supplies, and his team needs to find a way to get him what he needs. They need a solution quickly, as time is running out. The situation is dire. Jeff Daniels's character, playing NASA Director Teddy Sanders, suggests the unthinkable. Well . . . He doesn't suggest. He asks how often NASA's testing raises an error. The answer is one in twenty. Of course, the other characters immediately state, "You aren't suggesting we don't test, are you?" Daniels's character's response is "I'm just asking how often for now." Once that is answered, he asks the group, "Can you think of a safer way to create more time?"

No one can.

Now, I would be remiss if I didn't state that the tactic they rush fails. But just think: They potentially would have wasted ten more days by testing it. This was a situation in which failing fast helped them get to the right solution sooner. This example from *The Martian* showcases the concept of being curious and, at times, breaking from the norm with the added insight into the benefits of failing fast!

Since the test itself did not put a human life at more risk, this was a situation in which failing quickly due to not testing benefited Matt Damon's character. By testing, NASA would have discovered the same outcome, but it would have discovered that outcome ten days later—an amount of time it could not afford to waste. The result was that NASA could get busy working on a solution that would work instead of testing a failed hypothesis. This was possible because the director himself was willing to break from NASA's normal protocols and suggest the unthinkable with a curious question: "What if we didn't test?"

INCREASED EMPLOYEE ENGAGEMENT AND RETENTION

Cultivating a curiosity-driven leadership style prevents employees from letting their roles become boring or stagnant because it engages them in delving into questions and inquiring about new things. Enabling those in the business environment to continuously learn and develop keeps the work environment dynamic and stimulating. A curiosity-driven business environment encourages employees to come to work with positive energy rather than dread. Innovation and creativity are not just nurtured but celebrated. So, all employees are motivated to bring their best selves to work with the hope of being innovative and creative and making a difference because they both influence and are influenced by the creativity of others.

When management cultivates a business environment where curiosity is valued, employees are more likely to proactively make suggestions, propose ideas, and strategize in problem-solving, which can develop into breakthrough innovation. In this atmosphere of curiosity, there is less likelihood that new ideas will be withheld because people feel freer expressing their observations and asking questions. Open inquiry fosters a spirit of collaboration, where people feel comfortable sharing their knowledge and learning, thereby creating a rich, ongoing discourse of ideas and expertise.

Furthermore, job satisfaction is generally higher when employees feel they have a stake in decisions regarding how the business operates or where it's headed over the long term. They feel more empowered and take more pride in being part of the business. When employees see their contributions as a direct means to the company's success, it tells them that they should stick around and invest more time in the organization.

Empowered employees are also more invested in maintaining quality and excellence in the business. This has significant implications for employee loyalty and solidifies employees' trust in leadership. When employees see that the future of the business is open to their thoughts and ideas, and they see how their thoughts and ideas directly contribute to the company's successes, it helps strengthen their bonds with their work communities.

Fostering an environment where curiosity can flourish also requires providing the structures, resources, and institutional support through which employees can experiment, take risks, and learn from failures. In this way, organizations commit to their employees' professional growth and how this work will provide a basis for development across multiple areas of their lives. Organizations can create these structures via various avenues, including training and development programs, mentorship relationships, and opportunities for continuing education. Flexible working models, whether through temporary reassignments to other organizational units or projects that span function, allow employees to develop new skills and new ways of seeing the work of others in their company. When an organization creates such structures, it signals to its employees that it is committed to valuing them and supporting their professional development.

Simon Sinek has a video from a speech in which he discusses a hotel employee he met at a hotel he was staying in. However, this employee also worked at another hotel, and his work experiences were completely different. In one job, he felt appreciated and empowered because the managers were constantly asking how they could support their employees. At the other hotel, managers were constantly pointing out what was wrong. Sinek explains that in the latter job, employees are taught to keep their heads down, do the basics, minimize any errors, just collect their paychecks, and go home.

Unfortunately, I have learned about the importance of a positive culture more from environments of poor culture than environments with positive ones. I worked for a business that exemplified the exact same negative outcome that Sinek's hotel employee described. It was a very cutthroat environment that could best be described as toxic, and there were many different hurdles. Although the leadership saw management as driving results and innovation, management had actually created the opposite effect. This team taught staff to keep their heads down, do the very basics, and try their hardest to not get noticed. This kind of environment ensures that curiosity, creativity, and innovation will not be present. The main culprit goes back to the notion of psychological safety. The employees did not feel respected, let alone encouraged to embrace curiosity. What resulted? Extremely high turnover, often by employees the leadership thought were happy and engaged.

In sum, engagement and retention improve when curiosity is woven into the tapestry of the organization's culture. As an outcome, a committed, energized, forward-thinking workforce is created, and the company thrives.

Beyond the business advantage of having a curious workforce, however, there are implications for positively impacting employees' sense of work identity. Ultimately, if leaders spoke out loud to their people about their interest and respect for their learning appetite, such affirmation and validation would bring personal value to the employees' work and make their jobs more enjoyable. In the end, what is attractive to us in our working lives is an environment that makes us feel good to be part of it, where we bring out the best in ourselves, and where everyone is looking out for others' success. That's a win-win.

IMPROVED DECISION-MAKING AND STRATEGIC PLANNING

Investing in a culture of curiosity can help an organization make more effective decisions and plan better. When employees are welcome to ask questions and come from different perspectives, there is more diverse input. This helps employees make more comprehensive analyses, get a fuller picture of potential success factors, and have greater confidence in the decisions made.

For strategic planning, harnessed curiosity can be a great ally. Curious workers are more likely to engage in the creative thinking and problem-solving process that can recognize variables and scenarios that might have gone unnoticed under less curious circumstances. Curious workers are also more likely to offer valuable contributions by doing thorough research, identifying trends, and recognizing potential innovations. A curious workforce can be more capable of predicting movements in an industry and adapting strategies to weather challenges accordingly.

Curiosity allows organizations to fill the gaps and holes and build upon data-driven and operationally excellent foundations. Aspirational and visionary strategic planning is necessary for setting goals and plotting the course for long-term growth. However, it is important to make sure you first have the operational foundation to achieve those goals. Curiosity is the gateway to making that happen.

> **A curious workforce can be more capable of predicting movements in an industry and adapting strategies to weather challenges accordingly.**

Further, integrating curiosity into the strategic planning process encourages a proactive stance; rather than merely reacting to market shifts, curious organizations pursue improvements and new opportunities before those shifts occur. This creates more durable and adaptable plans and makes the organization more flexible when it comes to engaging with the vagaries of its own environment and the external world.

In turn, better decisions and strategic thinking can lead to a more energetic, empowered, and responsive organization. As long as interest-driven interrogation fuels it, it has enough time to settle and crystallize, and the affordances for innovation that collectively intelligent structures possess can help generate novel and robust strategies.

MEASURABLE BUSINESS GROWTH AND SUSTAINABILITY

When curiosity is formally integrated into the corporate culture, the resulting impact on measurable business results and long-term sustainability is undeniable. When creative thinking and inquisitive perspectives are explicitly welcomed and supported by senior leadership and the small, daily habits of employees, the organization unlocks new spaces for progressive productivity and profit. Performance measurements and benchmarks, such as revenue growth, market share expansion, or customer acquisition rates, can all be enhanced through a curious workforce committed to continuous improvement and innovation.

Furthermore, more curious companies are better positioned to adopt more sustainable practices, which benefit both the environment and sustainable profitability. Interested employees are more likely to identify resource-efficient practices, reduce waste, and create sustainable products and services that appeal to green-minded consumers.

Moreover, cultivating an exploratory culture can help foster greater employee engagement and retain talented individuals. People who feel liberated to discover and share new ideas will enjoy their roles and be less likely to look elsewhere for opportunities. Organizations benefit from the decrease in turnover as they can cut the costs associated with hiring and training new hires, and institutional knowledge is maintained.

Therefore, applying growth to accounting numbers and sustainable development will allow businesses to combine sensible rejuvenation of themselves through performance with sensible stewardship of themselves in terms of their community and the environment. The result is a robust, resilient, integrated system in which an enterprise can become stronger by nurturing its carrying environment while maintaining its competitive effectiveness.

CHAPTER 8
OVERCOMING BARRIERS TO CURIOSITY

*"I'm not interested in preserving the status quo;
I want to overthrow it."*
—Machiavelli

While fostering an organization-wide operation and culture of curiosity is a powerful leg in the quest to create a curious business, equally important is identifying and removing the barriers that can squash this valuable trait before it can even get off the ground. Fear, ego, and resistance are the biggest culprits to address. Fear of failure, fear of outright rejection, or even the fear of the unknown or the unfamiliar can freeze your workforce and prevent them from trying something new or coming up with different or innovative solutions.

Ego can interpose itself when employees are too invested in having it their way or are too attached to their ideas or achievements to open themselves to learning from others or admit they might not have all the answers.

And, finally, resistance of one kind or another—at the individual or organizational level—can present itself to block innovation when established routines and comfort zones are challenged and the incumbent occupiers of the status quo resist change. In this chapter, we discuss these three all-too-common barriers to curiosity and offer approaches to helping break them down so that your organization's potential for curiosity can be liberated.

IDENTIFYING AND ADDRESSING FEARS RELATED TO CURIOSITY

Fear is among the most substantial barriers to curious leadership. Fear of failure, of being looked at the wrong way, and of misplacing organizational resources can be driving forces behind leaders—and employees—who aim for narrow ways instead of being endangered. The enemies of fear are the desire to innovate further, experiment, and create new avenues. The perception that there is no room for failure and that it will result in shame, feeble performance, and consequent loss of jobs is an extreme error in organizational design. Therefore, the role of leaders and managers is to render fear inconsequential.

Four Types of Fears and Ways to Overcome Them

Fear is a natural and debilitating mental component when it comes to innovation, growth, and change.

Fear shows up in different forms, but at its core, fear can stifle innovation, silence important voices, and keep teams from reaching their full potential. I've seen it firsthand in many forms—whether it's fear of failing, fear of judgment, fear of resource allocation, or simply a lack of trust within the team.

I've encountered fear of failure time and again. Leaders and employees alike often hesitate to take risks because they're afraid of what might happen if things don't go as planned. I once worked with a team that had incredible potential for innovation, but they were paralyzed by the idea that if a new initiative didn't succeed, heads would roll. That fear kept them clinging to the status quo even though they knew it wasn't serving the organization. What turned things around was that leadership finally embraced the idea of failure being a part of the learning process—not an end but a step on the journey. When that cultural shift happened, the team began to experiment and, in doing so, found solutions they hadn't even imagined.

> **Fear can stifle innovation, silence important voices, and keep teams from reaching their full potential.**

There is no shortage of gurus, influencers, multimillionaires, and multibillionaires out there who talk down to those who follow them, calling them losers, failures, and sometimes even worse. They make it seem as though they have never not seen success, have never had doubts, or have never experienced fears. Their demeanors and bravado create this holier-than-thou approach to encouraging and motivating people. Here's the problem they miss: If someone is facing fear and self-doubt, this mentality will not work. There's that age-old anecdote of how you can hang around with five people of a certain quality and become the sixth. But that happens only when you have the right mindset and confidence. If you are mired in self-doubt, self-judgment, and fear, hearing from these influencers can make you feel less than as opposed to motivated.

Here is a piece of advice from an executive coach I worked with. Influencers, gurus, coaches, etc., are great at what they are talking about because they are shoveling their own shit. They're talking about the challenges they have faced and do face. Do not get caught up in the notion that there are people out there who don't have fear and are 100 percent confident all the time. Don't let them put you down for the place you're in because they have been there too. Get beyond the fear and just keep moving forward.

Fear of judgment is another big one. I've been in rooms where the hesitation to speak up was palpable. People were terrified that their ideas would be dismissed or criticized. I'll never forget a junior team member who pulled me aside after a meeting to share an idea they didn't feel comfortable voicing in the room. It turned out to be a game-changing insight, and I realized how much brilliance we were leaving on the table because we hadn't created a safe environment for everyone to contribute. To overcome this, leaders must model openness and vulnerability, showing their teams that it's not just okay to ask questions and push back—it's vital to the success of the organization.

Without trust, curiosity simply cannot thrive.

Then there's the fear of resource constraints. In resource-strapped environments, curiosity-driven projects are often seen as luxuries the organization can't afford. I've worked with leaders who believed that every penny and every minute had to be spent on necessity-driven projects, leaving no room for exploration or experimentation. But the truth is, some of the most impactful initiatives come from allowing a little room to explore the what-ifs. When organizations implement transparent processes to evaluate and prioritize projects, it becomes easier to balance the demands of necessity with the potential of curiosity.

Finally, there's the lack of trust. I've been in organizations where trust was so broken that employees were afraid to share ideas or speak candidly about challenges. Without trust, curiosity simply cannot thrive. To build trust, it takes consistent **effort from leaders—being transparent, following through on commitments, and creating open lines of communication.** One leader I worked with started holding weekly ask-me-anything sessions with their team. It was a simple gesture, but it signaled to everyone that their voices mattered and they could bring their questions and ideas forward without fear. Over time, that trust fostered an environment where curiosity flourished, **leading to innovations that transformed the organization.**

Addressing these fears isn't easy, but it's necessary. When leaders intentionally create a culture that sees failure as learning, values diverse perspectives, allocates resources strategically, and builds trust, they open the door for curiosity to drive real innovation. It's about showing teams that fear doesn't have to hold them back—that the greatest breakthroughs often come when we're willing to push past it and explore what lies on the other side.

INNOVATION POLICIES

Although fear and the other hurdles to curiosity are natural elements, it is important to move beyond fear to innovation, growth, and change. One way to get beyond our humanistic insecurities is to create policies that encourage curiosity on a regular basis. Two companies that exemplify this commitment are Google and 3M.

Before we get into that, I want to call out the elephant in the room here. It is easy to say, "Yeah, but they basically have endless resources. My small organization cannot compete with some of the richest companies in the world."

The question should be, Can they compete with you? There are many components of small organizations that make them more ripe for innovation, growth, and change. Small organizations are flatter, which allows for quicker decision-making, more collaboration, better 360-degree views of the organization, and more flexibility than larger companies. Even though Google and 3M are both extremely innovative companies, they are still machines with many moving parts, and they have bureaucracies that can hinder their ability to move as fast as small businesses. This was showcased in a recent World Economic Forum study.[16]

Much is said about Google's 20 percent time policy. This policy gives every employee at Google 20 percent of their working time—approximately one day a week—that they can spend on whatever they choose. The benefits of this free company time and creative freedom are shown in several cases where ideas for new products were born using this 20 percent time. For example, Google Maps was developed by a software engineer pursuing a hobby project to make a real-time map of road traffic using the infrastructure of Google Earth. Gmail started as a similar side project that quickly expanded to a widely used tool that millions rely on daily. The company created a culture of creativity and constantly brought new features and services to the market.

Similarly, 3M—a company that prides itself on innovation—has long had what it calls the 15 percent rule. This dictates that every employee should spend 15 percent of their working time on new ideas or projects. The 15 percent rule, which senior management is still committed to, was fundamental in establishing a culture where creativity wasn't just encouraged—it was expected. The Post-it note is a classic example of what can be achieved when 15 percent time is used to its fullest. When the 3M scientist wrote his famous note after struggling to find a strong adhesive, his 15 percent time was critical to the eventual market success of his adhesive and the company. The 15 percent rule has also been responsible for 3M's consistent success, allowing the firm to stay ahead in the highly competitive market by embedding an ethos of innovation into the fabric of the company.

RECOGNIZING THE IMPACT OF EGO ON CURIOSITY

It can be a potent suppressor of curiosity and an impediment to openness and innovation. If a leader's ego starts ruling the company, that leader will be less likely to consider other points of view or listen to the opinions of those around them. Innovation stagnates and team members lose motivation to put forth new thinking when leaders dismiss good ideas. And if they're chronically unhappy, team members are less likely to go out of their way to bring an idea to life for them. Bringing awareness to the effects that a leader's ego has on curiosity is a first step in thwarting their ego's impact on the enterprise.

Cultivating Humility and Openness to New Ideas

There is a need to balance an ego's restrictive presence in leadership by cultivating humility and openness. Humble leaders are comfortable acknowledging that they don't have all the answers or always know the correct course of action. They listen to and learn from other stakeholders. This creates a more inclusive, dynamic workplace where differences are valued rather than disregarded or suppressed. By practicing active listening, promoting teamwork, and appreciating fresh thinking, leaders can foster a culture of humility and openness.

Strategies for Reducing Ego-Driven Resistance

Downplaying ego-driven resistance includes techniques for encouraging self-awareness and a sense of teamwork. Leaders and employees can be prompted to employ self-reflection as a matter of course. Training for leaders and employees in emotional intelligence and conflict management disciplines could reduce ego-related habits and blind spots. Leaders can model vulnerability by talking about their struggles and setbacks since being fallible is permissible. Coordinating and overlapping projects and task assignments can provide opportunities for teammates to work together and experience the benefits of contributions. A culture of curiosity and innovation thrives when team members work on shared ideas and no one feels stigmatized.

> **By practicing active listening, promoting teamwork, and appreciating fresh thinking, leaders can foster a culture of humility and openness.**

Creating a curious culture and leadership style is a great way to combat ego in the workplace. Embracing a culture where everything can be challenged—even you—requires you to leave your ego at the door. There's no doubt that this is more easily said than done, but start by adopting some of the curious-culture mechanisms mentioned earlier in the book. Once you learn that empowering others through curiosity improves results, you will be more eager to step aside and adopt a more servant-leadership style, fostering the growth of others.

I have had my fair share of dealing with egos throughout my career. This includes executives and managers I worked under as well as facing my own ego in real time or in retrospect. Breaking down egos is very tough. If you are an executive who may worry if your ego is getting in the way of innovation, growth, and change, take a moment to see how your ego may be resisting ideas. If you are a rising star or manager who is tackling resistance from upper management, think about how you can soften the delivering and execution of new ideas, change, and innovation.

RESISTANCE

Resistance to curiosity comes from employees (and executives) who fear the unknown or losing their jobs, an organizational culture that rewards playing it safe over playing, and recent past experiences in which failing received a punishment rather than an opportunity to learn. Failing forward can help leaders break through these barriers. There are several examples and stories throughout this book that highlight the role leadership plays in encouraging or reducing curiosity. Creating a culture of fear by constantly pointing out mistakes instead of championing wins increases fear and creates the negative, heads-down culture mentioned earlier.

Tactics for Overcoming Organizational Inertia

Organizational inertia is like a stubborn boulder—heavy, immovable, and frustratingly resistant to a nudge in the right direction. I've seen it up close. Teams cling to the status quo because it feels familiar, safe, and predictable. But let's be honest: what got you here won't get you there.

The first step to breaking through this inertia is to get crystal clear on the "why." Teams need to understand how curiosity, experimentation, and innovation connect to the organization's bigger mission and goals. Now, I'm not trying to follow in Simon Sinek's footsteps here—I'll let him be the *Start with Why* guy—but I'll admit we seem to see culture and leadership through a very similar lens. If people don't understand why something matters, they're not going to care enough to change. Plain and simple.

When curiosity feels risky or disruptive, start small. Let your team run a few manageable experiments—nothing overwhelming, just tweaks to processes or tiny trials of new ideas. I've found this approach takes the pressure off. When people see those small wins, they start to realize curiosity isn't some abstract idea; it's a practical tool for progress. And progress builds momentum.

Here's where leadership makes a huge difference: Celebrate curiosity. When someone challenges the status quo, asks a bold question, or brings a fresh idea to the table, don't just give a quiet nod of approval. Call it out. Loudly. "That's a great question—let's explore that" can do wonders. Trust me, when you start recognizing curiosity in this way, it spreads. People feel safe speaking up, testing new ideas, and questioning the "way we've always done it."

I think the most simple thing is to allow questions, think of the unknown, and be curious!

And here's the final piece: equip your people. Curiosity isn't just about permission—it's about preparation. Give your team the tools, training, and space they need to engage in curiosity without fear. Maybe it's time for brainstorming workshops, innovation challenges, or even just creating pockets of time for exploration. Whatever it looks like, make curiosity part of the day-to-day rhythm.

Overcoming inertia doesn't mean you need a grand plan or sweeping changes overnight. It just takes consistent, intentional effort. The reality is, as leaders, we set the tone. If we embrace curiosity, reward experimentation, and show that it's okay to ask, "What if?" our teams will follow. And that's when the magic happens. Curiosity stops being a disruption and becomes the engine for growth, innovation, and change.

When You Are the Problem

As leaders, we often focus on identifying barriers within our teams, systems, or organizations. But sometimes, the most significant barrier to curiosity and innovation isn't external—it's us. Recognizing this isn't an admission of failure; it's an opportunity to grow.

I'll never forget leading a workshop for an organization that was struggling with innovation and collaboration. During one of the exercises, participants were encouraged to share their thoughts openly and without judgment. The goal was to foster a safe space for curiosity and exploration. However, as the discussion unfolded, the organization's EVP interrupted to publicly call out a staff member, harshly questioning their perspective. The room went silent. The energy shifted from open engagement to fear and discomfort.

What became clear in that moment was that the EVP was part of the problem, if not a major piece to the problem. When we first spoke, everything was about others' perception, but her perception came out in the meeting. As the workshop progressed, there was a lot of animosity. Then the group discussed a specific workplace policy, and the EVP criticized the staff for following it because, in her opinion, the staff weren't doing enough, though complying. In this situation, who is the best person to resolve this issue? She didn't like the policy and attacked the team instead of changing it.

This experience taught me a valuable lesson: as leaders, we have to consistently reflect on whether our own actions or attitudes are stifling the very curiosity we aim to cultivate. Even with the best intentions, we can unintentionally create environments where employees feel hesitant to speak up, challenge assumptions, or propose new ideas. It also led me to have a deeper initial mini workshop with the POC so we knew truly where the issues lay, even if with them.

The first step in addressing this is self-awareness. Here are some signs that you might be the barrier to curiosity within your organization:

- **You react defensively to new ideas:** If your first response is to dismiss, critique, or question the validity of an idea, you might be discouraging exploration.
- **You dominate conversations:** When leaders consistently take up the most airtime, it can signal that other perspectives aren't valued.
- **You prioritize hierarchy over collaboration:** If decisions are always made from the top down, employees may feel their input doesn't matter.
- **You're quick to assign blame:** Mistakes are inevitable in any organization. When leaders focus on blame rather than solutions, they create a culture of fear.

When leaders embrace the possibility that they might be the problem, they unlock the potential for profound transformation—not just for themselves, but for their teams. By addressing our own barriers, we create an environment where curiosity can thrive, ideas can flourish, and innovation becomes a natural byproduct of the culture we cultivate.

On a very personal note, I have often weaved this into my parenting. As a self-employed individual and entrepreneur, I do not work a nine-to-five. I often work into the evenings, jump on a call in the middle of the day, etc. Although I do my best to be present with my family, there are certainly times they bleed together. There are times I'm short, not attentive, or respond poorly in some other way. In order to keep my legitimacy with my son while asking him to own his mood, behaviors, etc., I have to do the same. I have no problems telling my son when I am the reason for my actions instead of pushing off blame or making excuses.

Being a curious leader isn't about being perfect—it's about being open. Open to feedback, open to change, and most importantly, open to the idea that we are always learning.

Leveraging Change Management Principles to Foster Curiosity

Change is hard—there's no sugarcoating that. And when you're asking people to embrace curiosity and question "the way we've always done it," it can feel downright disruptive. But here's the thing: curiosity thrives on change, and change doesn't have to be scary or overwhelming when handled with intention.

The first step is simple: talk to your team. Be transparent about *why* building a culture of curiosity matters. How does it align with your organization's goals? What's the benefit for everyone involved? Think of it as building a bridge between curiosity and the broader mission. If your team understands the why behind the change, they're far more likely to embrace it.

Once the message is clear, you'll need allies. You can't champion curiosity alone. Find the people in your organization who are already asking the big questions or bringing fresh ideas to the table—those curiosity pioneers who can help lead the way. Having these voices on board builds credibility and momentum. When people see curiosity in action, led by peers they trust, they're much more likely to join in.

It's also on us as leaders to make the environment feel *safe* for curiosity to flourish. That means creating a culture where exploring new ideas is supported and celebrated—not nitpicked or criticized. I've seen it time and again: when people feel they can experiment without fear of failure or punishment, they unlock incredible potential. But here's the catch—resistance will show up. Change always invites it. Whether it's fear of the unknown, a reluctance to let go of old habits, or just plain skepticism, some people will push back. Instead of ignoring it, lean in. Listen. Understand where the resistance is coming from, and include those voices in the process.

Here's where vision meets action: Don't try to flip the whole system overnight. Start small. Curiosity doesn't require a grand, sweeping initiative on day one. Introduce curiosity-driven experiments—like dedicating time in team meetings to explore questions or trying low-risk pilot projects. Gradually build in feedback loops so you can gather insights and adjust as you go. These small wins are powerful because they prove that curiosity works. Over time, they build confidence and momentum, turning skeptics into advocates.

But the real magic comes in sustaining the change. Curiosity can't be a one-and-done initiative. It has to become part of the rhythm of the organization. This means continually reinforcing it through communication, recognition, and opportunities to grow. Celebrate those moments when someone asks a bold question or tries something new—even if it doesn't work perfectly. Reward effort, not just outcomes. Show that curiosity isn't just tolerated; it's *valued*.

At its core, curiosity is a muscle that grows stronger with practice. As leaders, we're the trainers. If we communicate the vision, build support systems, and make curiosity a safe and rewarding habit, we'll see it take root and transform the culture.

So, let's get to it. Be clear. Be supportive. And above all, be curious.

CHAPTER 9

IMMEDIATE ACTIONABLE STEPS FOR LEADING WITH CURIOSITY

"When people lack curiosity, they dismiss new opportunities instead of taking the time to explore them."
—Gary Vaynerchuk

CLEAR YOUR MIND FOR INNOVATION

Creating a mindset conducive to innovation begins with the ability to clear your mind of preconceptions and biases. By practicing mindfulness and reflective thinking, you can approach challenges with a fresh perspective, unhampered by the constraints of past experiences or rigid beliefs. Incorporating regular moments of reflection allows you to question your vision and examine if it still aligns with your organization's evolving goals. Maintaining mental clarity ensures that you stay open to new ideas and perspectives, fostering a creative environment where novel solutions can flourish.

Michael A. Singer is best known as a spiritual teacher and author, particularly for his books *The Untethered Soul* and *The Surrender Experiment*, both of which explore themes of inner peace, mindfulness, and the power of surrendering to life's flow. *The Untethered Soul* has become a popular guide for those interested in self-discovery and spiritual growth—people who are focusing on letting go of mental clutter and connecting with their deeper consciousness. The book gained significant attention and was even endorsed by Oprah Winfrey, who broadened its reach.

Mindfulness and letting go are areas I have been working on. As an operations professional, I had to make things happen. It was my job to solve the problem, get the program launched, etc. But here's what my spiritual journey has taught me: You can't make results happen. You can only do the work and let the results occur.

The Surrender Experiment was about Singer's willingness to let go and take on what opportunities were brought to him. It was about not saying no to the universe. You might be thinking, *Sure, it's easy for a yogi—a spiritual guru who lives in a spiritual commune—to let go and accept what comes.* But he is a very successful entrepreneur. The property where he conducts his spiritual and meditative practices, The Temple of the Universe, consists of six hundred acres. Singer did not set out to own this large plot of land. He actually was looking to get away from everyone. But it just kind of grew. He launched a multimillion-dollar construction company and kept buying land when the opportunities arose. He also taught himself to code and launched Medical Manager, which WebMD later acquired for $5 billion—all because he was willing to let go, believe in his abilities, and take on opportunities that arose.

QUESTIONING EVERYTHING: LEAVING NO STONE UNTURNED

To lead with curiosity means to embrace a mindset of relentless inquiry, where every assumption is challenged and every possibility is explored. This approach requires questioning the status quo and examining all aspects of a problem, leaving no stone unturned. By adopting an inquisitive attitude, leaders and employees can uncover hidden opportunities, identify potential risks, and generate innovative solutions that drive the organization forward. Encouraging teams to ask the right questions and delve deeper into issues fosters a culture of continuous improvement and discovery. This relentless pursuit of knowledge propels growth and ensures that the organization remains adaptable and resilient in the face of change.

> **Encouraging teams to ask the right questions and delve deeper into issues fosters a culture of continuous improvement and discovery.**

Toyota provides an extraordinary example of what it means to embody the principle of questioning everything and leaving no stone unturned. At the heart of its philosophy lies *kaizen*, a Japanese term that translates to "change for better." This is more than just a methodology—it's a mindset embedded deep in Toyota's culture, encouraging employees at every level to constantly examine processes, identify inefficiencies, and propose improvements. For Toyota, it's not about perfection but about continuous iteration, always moving closer to excellence.

Caterpillar has adopted Toyota's principles. Since it has a factory in my hometown, I am very familiar with Caterpillar and once visited its facility. I left inspired. It was remarkable to see how this company empowered every employee, from frontline workers to managers, to actively question the status quo.

On Toyota's production lines, there's a system called Andon, which allows any worker to stop the production process if they detect an issue. Imagine the courage and trust it takes to give that level of authority to every individual. Yet Toyota believes that solving problems at the root, in the moment, prevents larger inefficiencies down the line. It's an act of questioning with purpose—of refusing to accept good enough when better is always within reach.

Toyota's commitment to minimizing waste is another hallmark of its approach. Its lean manufacturing system, part of the Toyota Production System (TPS), relentlessly examines every aspect of its operations, from assembly lines to supply chain logistics. Whether it's wasted time, materials, or motion, nothing escapes scrutiny. This attention to detail keeps inefficiencies from snowballing into bigger issues. Even when Toyota faced major recalls in the early 2010s, it didn't shy away from hard questions. Instead, it doubled down on its *kaizen* philosophy, reevaluating quality control measures and ensuring that its processes were even more resilient.

What makes Toyota's approach so powerful is its adaptability. It has proven that questioning everything doesn't just lead to operational excellence. It creates a culture of resilience and growth. While other companies might crumble under external pressures, Toyota's relentless focus on improvement allows it to learn, adapt, and emerge stronger. It's no wonder organizations worldwide have adopted *kaizen* as a model for striving for efficiency and innovation. Toyota's story is a reminder that questioning isn't just a tool for solving problems—it's a way of thinking that drives success.

We can all appreciate the complex systems that Toyota and Caterpillar have to have in place, and it's amazing that they are able to adopt these types of principles. But it begs the question, If factories and companies with thousands of employees, complex systems, state-of-the-art manufacturing, and never-ending supply chains can adopt such principles, why can't more small businesses, startups, and nonprofits do the same?

The answer is that they absolutely can.

Lifting every stone has been a hallmark of my career. Having launched or managed operations for over a dozen organizations, I know firsthand how resistant many CEOs are, but I also understand the importance of getting beyond that resistance. My career has encompassed an ability to analyze and question. But I've done that from a place of helping and honesty. When my operations career began to take off, I thought that honesty and understanding were crucial because I was a trusted ally to the CEO. My questions and insistence on change were solely for the organization's benefit. Of course, this doesn't mean I never overstepped or made mistakes. I most certainly did. But looking back at my career, I can see that my impact and the changes I helped bring about by asking simple and hard questions made all the difference.

FRESH PERSPECTIVES AND DIVERSE INPUTS

Encouraging contributions from all levels of the organization is paramount for fostering innovation. This involves creating a culture where team members feel safe and actively invited to share their ideas and perspectives. Leaders should host regular forums, such as town hall meetings, discussion panels, and innovation sprints, dedicated solely to sharing ideas. Implementing suggestion boxes and anonymous feedback channels (criticized earlier in the book) can be the start while you're working to build trust, but feedback loops must go deeper and be more transparent. Additionally, ensuring representation from diverse demographics, including different departments, backgrounds, and experience levels, will enrich the ideation process. Leaders should demonstrate openness by actively engaging with these perspectives, providing timely feedback, and integrating viable ideas into actionable plans. Recognizing and rewarding contributions will further nurture a culture of inclusivity and innovation.

Warby Parker is an inspiring example of a smaller company that thrives on fostering fresh perspectives and diverse inputs. From its very beginning, the eyewear retailer set out to challenge the traditional industry by thinking differently, not just about its products but about how it engaged its people and customers.

I was first exposed to Warby Parker when a client of mine did some work with it. I hadn't yet seen its stores and commercials. One thing that struck me when I first learned about Warby Parker was how much it values every voice in the organization. Whether you are a store associate on the floor or sitting in the executive suite, your ideas matter. I once heard a story about how feedback from store employees—those who interact with customers every day—led to meaningful changes in the way stores were laid out, making the shopping experience smoother and more enjoyable for customers. It's the kind of environment where people feel like their insights can make an impact, and that kind of openness doesn't just happen—it's intentional.

What also stands out about Warby Parker is how it took inspiration from unexpected places to disrupt the eyewear industry. Its founders didn't just look at what other eyewear companies were doing. They pulled ideas from emerging online retail trends and the growing direct-to-consumer movement in other industries. The result? A completely new approach to buying glasses, with features like affordable pricing, the ability to try frames at home, and a commitment to giving back through the company's social mission. It wasn't just selling glasses. It was redefining how people thought about purchasing them.

Warby Parker also thrives on collaboration. It regularly brings together people from different departments—marketing, tech, retail, and customer service—to work on major projects. This cross-functional teamwork means new initiatives are shaped by a wide variety of perspectives. Take Warby Parker's virtual try-on feature, for example. More than the tech team was behind it; insights from retail and customer service staff played a key role in ensuring that this feature meets real customer needs. That feature has become one of the company's standout innovations, making it easier for customers to find the perfect pair of glasses from the comfort of their homes.

And perhaps most impressively, Warby Parker listens. Really listens. It's constantly seeking input from its customers—whether through surveys, social media, or other channels—and using that feedback to shape products and services. The result is a brand that feels modern and innovative as well as deeply connected to the people it serves. Customers know their voices matter, and that connection has built a fiercely loyal following.

Warby Parker shows us that you don't have to be a massive corporation to embrace diverse perspectives and fresh ideas.

It's a reminder that no matter the size of your company, staying open, collaborative, and customer-focused can lead to incredible innovation and success.

GATHERING DATA: PRESENT AND FUTURE

Arming yourself with detailed data is crucial for informed decision-making. This involves both an in-depth evaluation of current operations and a continuous scanning of emerging industry trends. Quantitative data—such as performance metrics, sales figures, and financial reports—provides a solid foundation for understanding where the organization currently stands. Complementing this with qualitative data gathered from customer feedback, employee surveys, and market research delivers a holistic view. Leveraging advanced analytics and business intelligence tools can help in processing and interpreting this data, revealing underlying patterns and insights. Additionally, staying abreast of technological advancements, regulatory changes, and competitive moves ensures that an organization can anticipate and adapt to future disruptions. Regularly updating this data and adjusting strategies accordingly will position the organization to innovate proactively rather than reactively.

A great example of a smaller company doing exactly that is Casper, the direct-to-consumer mattress company. Casper has leveraged data collection from both current and potential customers to inform its marketing, product development, and long-term growth strategies.

When Casper launched in 2014, it completely reimagined the traditional mattress industry. Instead of navigating the awkward and often overwhelming experience of buying a mattress in a store, Casper offered a fresh, direct-to-consumer approach. Mattresses arrived in a box that was conveniently delivered to your door. Beyond just a novel delivery system, Casper built a brand that resonated deeply with modern consumers—one focused on simplicity, accessibility, and trust. But what really set Casper apart was how it leaned into data collection and analysis to fuel its growth and innovation.

From the start, Casper was relentless in gathering customer feedback. I've always been impressed by how it used that information as a way to not just resolve complaints but to shape its products. Every return, every review, and every comment became a data point for improvement. If customers said a mattress was too firm or wore out too quickly, Casper refined the design. This real-time feedback loop wasn't just good for customer satisfaction—it directly reduced return rates, which is no small feat in an industry where comfort is subjective and returns can eat into profits.

Casper's marketing is another area where data played a pivotal role. The company didn't just launch campaigns and hope for the best. It studied the data. It tracked click-through rates, analyzed conversion metrics, and segmented its audience based on demographics and behavior. One thing that stood out to me was how Casper identified that content about sleep health resonated strongly with its audience. It leaned into this insight, creating targeted campaigns that focused on the importance of quality sleep, which boosted ad performance and solidified the company's identity as a brand that cares about its customers' well-being.

As Casper grew, it began using data to expand its product line in a way that felt both natural and strategic. It started with mattresses, but as it listened to customers and studied market trends, it realized there was a demand for complementary products, like pillows, bed frames, and sleep accessories. By introducing these items, Casper tapped into a broader market and built a more holistic sleep experience. It wasn't just about selling a mattress anymore. It was about creating a brand that owned the entire sleep category.

This data-driven mindset also informed geographic expansion. Casper analyzed website traffic and customer inquiries to identify international markets with high demand. By forecasting interest and targeting regions strategically, it expanded into Canada and Europe, making moves that were both calculated and highly effective.

One of the most exciting ways Casper uses data is in shaping the future of its products. By analyzing sleep patterns and conducting surveys, the company is not just thinking about today's customers—it's planning for what's next. It's clear that Casper is positioning itself not just as a mattress company but as a leader in sleep wellness, innovating based on how people's habits and needs evolve.

Casper's story is a testament to how a smaller company can leverage data to innovate, adapt, and grow. It didn't just disrupt an industry. It reinvented what it means to connect with customers and deliver products that fit their lives. It's a powerful reminder that when you're willing to listen, learn, and act on what you hear, the possibilities for growth are endless.

IMPACT AND OUTCOMES

Casper's ability to gather and apply data for both immediate and future needs has enabled it to become one of the most recognized brands in the direct-to-consumer mattress industry. By continuously refining its products and expanding thoughtfully into new areas, Casper has driven customer loyalty and increased its market share. This data-driven approach helps Casper stay agile in a competitive market and adapt to changing consumer expectations.

I once worked with a small company that reminded me of Casper's approach to data—a brand that transformed the mattress industry by listening deeply to its customers and anticipating their needs. Casper didn't just rely on one snapshot of customer feedback. Instead, it continually gathered data from every source possible—product reviews, website traffic, even sleep surveys—to gain a complete picture of what customers wanted.

I helped a company adopt a similar approach, encouraging its leadership to blend quantitative metrics with customer insights. It was a game-changer. Like Casper, it used this data to refine its product line, optimize marketing, and even pinpoint international markets ready for expansion. By continuously adapting based on data, this company didn't just stay relevant—it was able to predict and meet future customer needs.

Casper's story proves that gathering present data while scanning future trends isn't just for industry giants. It's a scalable strategy that any company can use to create loyalty, increase market share, and build a brand that thrives in any market.

I was once faced with a team that did not understand their data. It was one of those times when I was brought in to turn things around. This marketing department was responsible for more than 80 percent of the company's revenue through digital and direct-mail marketing. At the time, we had a non-marketing interim director overseeing the department. They were there for leadership and managerial purposes. The interim came to my office one day and said, "I need you to come to this meeting. I don't really know what's wrong here, but something isn't adding up." So I attended the meeting, where the person responsible for the data started talking about where we were to date. But she quickly followed it up with, "But there's no reason to worry. It's not that bad."

Well, I pulled out my phone to use my calculator and started running the numbers. What she was describing (though not **defining with proper forecasting) was that the current data** was showing that we were going to be 15 percent under revenue from an already very tight budget. Her response was, "That sounds about right."

The problem was that this individual did not understand all the data and its repercussions. The shortfall equated to 50 percent of our annual payroll budget. And this organization **had just laid off half its staff before bringing me on. It is not** hard to see how that trend would have continued if I had not asked serious and hard questions and gotten a hold of the data and numbers.

SETTING A STRATEGIC PATH

Once you have a refreshed mindset and a wealth of data, it's time to set a strategic path for your new direction. This involves crafting a comprehensive, actionable road map that encompasses both your long-term vision and the short-term steps required to achieve it.

Start by delineating clear objectives and key results that align with your overall mission. Break these down into manageable **milestones with specified timelines and resource allocations.** Ensure that this road map is transparent, is communicated effectively across the organization, and includes feedback loops for continuous learning and adaptation. Incorporate flexibility to accommodate shifting priorities and emerging insights. Establish regular check-ins and review sessions to track progress, celebrate wins, and address any roadblocks promptly. This strategic path should serve as a living document that evolves with the organization's growth and the dynamic external environment.

Leading with curiosity isn't a one-time initiative but an ongoing commitment to questioning, learning, and growing. By embracing these immediate, actionable steps, leaders and employees can create environments where innovation, change, and growth are natural outcomes. With an insatiable thirst for knowledge and a willingness to evolve, organizations can navigate any disruption with agility, resilience, and success. Stay curious and don't be afraid to challenge the status quo. This will drive your organization toward a brighter future.

I once worked with a small company that was in a similar position; it had gathered customer insights and looked at industry trends, and it was ready to make big changes. But with all the information on hand, the challenge became *how* to transform it into an actionable, focused plan.

We began by setting a clear, achievable vision. We broke down that vision into actionable goals, creating specific objectives and key results that directly aligned with the company's core mission. I encouraged the team to build manageable milestones and realistic timelines—something I learned firsthand when I was guiding a larger team years before. In that previous role, we set big, ambitious goals that sounded great on paper. But, without clear steps and timelines, they quickly felt overwhelming. So, with this smaller company, we decided to break goals into chunks, assigning clear timelines and resources to keep the team energized and on track.

Once the road map was defined, the focus shifted to making sure it was transparent and adaptable. We communicated the strategy across the organization—not just as a presentation but by opening up regular feedback channels so everyone could share their ideas and voice any concerns. There was a time in my own work experience when our road map was rigid and any new ideas were put on hold until the next cycle. This experience taught me the importance of flexibility. So, with this company, we built feedback loops that allowed the team to revisit the road map, update strategies, and incorporate new insights along the way. That flexibility allowed the team to quickly adapt when priorities shifted or new data emerged.

> **Don't be afraid to question the status quo. Let curiosity guide your organization toward a brighter, more innovative future.**

We held regular check-ins to track progress and celebrate small wins, creating momentum and keeping spirits high. In a project early in my career, I learned the power of celebrating small milestones. By acknowledging progress and addressing roadblocks, we kept morale up even during challenging times. With this small client company, the routine review sessions helped everyone feel connected to the strategy and empowered to push forward even when we hit rough patches.

This strategic path became a living document, evolving with the organization's growth and the ever-changing industry. The team learned that leading with curiosity isn't a one-time exercise but an ongoing commitment to questioning, learning, and growing. When leaders and employees embrace these steps—setting clear goals, staying adaptable, and keeping curiosity alive—innovation, change, and growth become part of the organizational fabric. As I've seen time and again, this approach enables an organization to navigate disruption with resilience, agility, and purpose. Don't be afraid to question the status quo. Let curiosity guide your organization toward a brighter, more innovative future.

This is exactly what we do on a daily basis at my consulting firm. We don't create strategies on nice-to-haves and wishful thinking. We dive into the operational analysis as previously explained, create a plan to execute, then coach our clients on mindset, execution, and culture. We bring all the elements that I talk about in this book in a succinct process that drives innovation, growth, and change.

EMBRACING FAILURE: LEARNING FROM MISTAKES

In a curious and innovative mindset, failure is seen not as an end but as a learning opportunity. Instead of fearing failure or avoiding risks, leaders must encourage their teams to experiment and explore different avenues, even if they may not result in immediate success. By embracing failure and approaching it with curiosity, individuals can identify what went wrong and use that knowledge to improve future endeavors. This also fosters a culture of psychological safety, where employees feel comfortable taking risks and sharing their ideas without fear of judgment or retribution. In this way, failure becomes a means for growth and progress rather than a hindrance.

A smaller company that has exemplified setting a strategic path effectively is Innocent Drinks, a smoothie and juice company based in the UK. Founded in 1999, Innocent built its brand by focusing on natural ingredients, sustainable practices, and a fun, approachable image. Its strategic path has helped it grow from a small startup to one of the leading smoothie brands in Europe.

Key Elements of Innocent's Strategic Path

Innocent Drinks is a fascinating example of a company that built its success by staying true to a clear and intentional strategic path. From the very beginning, its founders were determined to create a brand that stood for more than just selling beverages. They carved out the company's niche in the competitive drink market by focusing on three core values: natural ingredients, sustainability, and a relatable, playful brand identity. These values didn't just guide their decisions—they became the heart and soul of everything Innocent does.

What struck me about Innocent's story is how unwavering it's been in its commitment to simplicity and transparency. From day one, it made a promise to use only natural ingredients, avoiding preservatives and artificial additives. In a market flooded with sugary, overprocessed drinks, this wasn't just a differentiator—it was a bold statement. Innocent wasn't trying to be trendy. It was simply building trust with health-conscious consumers who were tired of wading through confusing labels. It's easy to see how this authenticity became a cornerstone of its success.

Sustainability is another area where Innocent leads with intention. Long before it became mainstream, this company was making strides to reduce its environmental impact. It was among the first in its industry to switch to 100 percent recyclable bottles and source ingredients ethically. This wasn't just a marketing tactic—it was a reflection of the company's genuine commitment to doing business responsibly. It's no surprise that this resonated deeply with customers who value eco-friendly practices, giving Innocent a distinct edge in a crowded market.

But what I love most about Innocent is its brand identity. It doesn't just sell smoothies. It's created a personality that feels approachable, fun, and even a little quirky. The packaging is a perfect example: You'll find humorous little messages that make you smile as you're reaching for its product in the store. Innocent has also been intentional about involving its customers in charitable projects, making people feel like they're part of something bigger. This kind of connection goes beyond transactions—it builds loyalty and makes customers feel like they're supporting a brand that genuinely cares.

Innocent's growth has also been fueled by its purpose-driven approach to business. It's made giving back a priority, donating a portion of profits to the Innocent Foundation, which supports various charitable causes. It's clear this isn't just a box to be checked—it's part of what Innocent is as a company. And that kind of authenticity has strengthened its reputation and deepened customer loyalty, helping the organization stand tall even in the face of much larger competitors.

Innocent Drinks reminds us that success doesn't have to come at the expense of values. By staying true to its core principles and embracing a sense of purpose, it has created a brand that thrives in the market and resonates with people on a deeper level. This is a testament to the power of building a company that knows exactly what it stands for—and isn't afraid to show it.

Impact of Innocent's Strategic Path

Innocent Drinks is a prime example of what happens when a company sets a clear vision and stays true to it. From the very beginning, Innocent carved out its place in the market by focusing on health, sustainability, and a brand identity that felt refreshingly different from the rest of the beverage industry. What's remarkable is how it managed to grow from a small UK-based company to one of the most recognized smoothie and juice brands across Europe, all while staying rooted in its core values.

What stands out about Innocent's journey is its ability to expand while keeping its identity intact. Even after catching the attention of Coca-Cola, which eventually acquired a majority stake in the company, Innocent continued to operate with autonomy, maintaining the playful, approachable vibe that made it so beloved in the first place. It's rare for a smaller company to navigate a partnership like that without losing its soul, but Innocent managed to do just that.

What really makes Innocent special is the deep connection it has fostered with its customers. This is a brand people don't just buy—they believe in it. The company's commitment to transparency, sustainability, and fun has built an emotional loyalty that goes far beyond the products themselves. It's not just about selling smoothies. It's about creating a community around values. That connection is what has kept Innocent competitive in an industry dominated by much larger players.

This story proves that you don't need to sacrifice what you stand for to grow. By sticking to its strategic path and focusing on what it does best, Innocent has scaled sustainably, earned the trust of its customers, and shown that even smaller companies can compete—and win—on a global stage.

Early in my career, I learned that the way we approach mistakes can make or break innovation. I worked for a startup where two executives had very different philosophies on risk and failure. One would often say, "No mistakes. We only have one chance to get this right." The pressure was intense; any error felt like a disaster, and everyone held back ideas that might rock the boat. It was a culture of fear, not creativity. Another executive, however, had a completely different view: "We can make all the mistakes we want as long as they happen within these walls." This leader encouraged us to test ideas, take calculated risks, and view failures as stepping-stones to improvement. That simple shift changed everything; the team felt safe to try, fail, and ultimately innovate.

This experience taught me that true growth requires embracing failure as part of the process. As Winston Churchill once said, "Success is going from failure to failure without loss of enthusiasm."[17] Innovation, growth, and change will always come with risks, and the most effective leaders recognize that some failures are inevitable on the path to progress. When we create an environment where people feel safe to take those risks, we open the door to greater creativity and resilience.

True growth requires embracing failure as part of the process.

As I progressed in my career and oversaw teams and even my own company, I learned to focus on growth, potential, problem-solving, and creativity as opposed to perfection. Perfection is an illusion. I've worked with leaders who did not suffer fools and would call out any kind of mistake. Here's the problem with mistakes: People who believe there should be no mistakes do not suffer such from others. But when they make a mistake, it's "I can't believe I did that."

This reminds me of the interview between Tony Robbins and Theo Von titled "Finding What You're Looking For: The Power of Belief." In this interview, Robbins asks Von to look around the room and spot things of a specific color (let's say red). After Von looks at many different objects, Robbins asks him what he saw of a different color (let's say blue). He was unable to identify anything for the second color. The point is that we find what we are looking for and not what we aren't.

> A curious culture isn't a nice-to-have—it's the difference between staying ahead of the curve and getting left behind.

Robbins even goes on to point out that Von likely even made some rationalizations. Does a maroon or orangish color become red if we're looking for red? This also shows how we manage teams and the kind of culture we build. If we think someone is a failure, we find mistakes. When we think someone is an A-player, we find ways to justify not seeing their mistakes. The key is to remain open, understand that mistakes happen, and *help* individuals grow and achieve more.

So, as you set a strategic path and embrace a culture of curiosity, remember that failure isn't the enemy—it's a tool. Each setback is a chance to learn, refine, and come back stronger. The more you foster this mindset, the more your team can use every lesson to drive meaningful, lasting success. Embrace the questions, celebrate the experiments, and keep moving forward.

CURIOSITY IN ACTION: SUSTAINING THE MOMENTUM

Curiosity isn't just a tool to solve today's challenges—it's the foundation for navigating tomorrow's unknowns. To thrive in a rapidly changing business landscape, leaders must foster a culture where curiosity fuels continuous learning, listening, and growth. This isn't about having all the answers; it's about encouraging everyone in the organization to ask better questions.

When leaders embrace curiosity, they make space for diverse perspectives, bold experiments, and innovative solutions. They create teams that adapt quickly, anticipate disruptions, and actively pursue new opportunities for growth. A curious culture isn't a nice-to-have—it's the difference between staying ahead of the curve and getting left behind.

So, as you move forward, remember this: Leading with curiosity means showing up with a willingness to question, learn, and explore every day. Keep asking. Keep listening. And most importantly, keep challenging the status quo.

Because when we lead with curiosity, we don't just solve problems—we open doors to possibilities we never imagined.

Let's get to it. Be curious, stay curious, and let's build something better—together.

CONCLUSION

CURIOSITY IN ACTION—DRIVING INNOVATION, GROWTH, AND CHANGE

> *"Curiosity cultivates change, fueling growth and innovation."*
> —Jon Bassford

Curiosity isn't just an inherent trait or a passive desire to learn—it's an active leadership style that can transform organizations from the inside out. Leaders who embody curiosity don't just ask questions. They put systems in place that encourage exploration, honest feedback, and continuous learning. Through a culture that values curiosity, organizations cultivate an environment where risk-taking and feedback are woven into the fabric of daily work, fueling sustainable growth and innovation.

As I've worked to integrate curiosity into my leadership style, I've come to realize that it's a continuous process. Early in my career, I worked on a high-stakes project where I felt enormous pressure to get everything right on the first try. My instinct was to stick with what I knew best instead of exploring new solutions. That fixed mindset led to a final result that fell short of what we could have achieved if I'd taken more time to ask questions and experiment. I walked away from that experience realizing that my reluctance to question the approach limited the outcome. That failure taught me that curiosity isn't about always having the right answers—it's about staying open to possibilities.

THE GROWTH MINDSET SHIFT: TRANSFORMING HOW YOU AND YOUR TEAM LEARN

Living curiosity as a leader begins with a growth mindset shift. Leaders who believe their team's potential is static won't achieve lasting change. Embracing a growth mindset is about rethinking challenges, seeing failures as learning opportunities, and fostering an environment where improvement is prioritized over perfection.

OPERATIONS EXCELLENCE: BUILDING CURIOSITY INTO PROCESSES

For curiosity to thrive, your operations need to be structured to allow for exploration. This means questioning existing processes, adopting agile practices, and creating a safe space for experimentation. The more curiosity becomes embedded in daily work, the more your team feels empowered to try new approaches, leading to increased efficiency, adaptability, and innovation.

CREATING A CURIOUS CULTURE: FOSTERING AN ENVIRONMENT WHERE CURIOSITY THRIVES

Ultimately, cultivating curiosity means building a culture where questioning is encouraged at all levels. Leaders can foster this by celebrating curiosity-driven successes, encouraging employees to speak up, and promoting a safe space for taking risks.

CALL TO ACTION FOR LEADERS TO EMBRACE CURIOSITY

I've learned that curiosity is more than just a trait—it's a practice. I've worked with leaders who fearlessly challenged assumptions, asking questions like "What if we're wrong?" or "What would we do if we weren't afraid to fail?" Those questions made the room feel more open and collaborative, and every team member felt encouraged to share their ideas. These experiences taught me that leaders can and should actively foster curiosity.

It's up to you, as a leader, to create an environment where curiosity is not only allowed but expected. Prioritize open dialogue, make space for dissenting ideas, and build a foundation of psychological safety that encourages team members to explore new possibilities. This mindset will unlock hidden potential in your team, setting a foundation for growth, innovation, and long-term success.

LEADERSHIP AND CURIOSITY ARE A PROCESS

Throughout this book, I have highlighted many successes and failures of organizations that I have worked for and with, as well as some well-known examples. Cultivating leadership and curiosity is a journey for everyone, and I am not an exception. Along the way, I have made many mistakes. This was showcased when I was pushing change too much instead of helping bring it about. Times when I overstepped my bounds in ways that hindered my potential, hurt relationships, and jeopardized jobs.

There are times when doing something the right way can still create confusing, if not negative, situations. One of the organizations in which I was brought in for enormous change inevitably felt a lot of uncertainty and, at times, hostility. As the old saying goes, you can't make an omelet without cracking an egg. An example I have given throughout is breaking down a department and manager. In addressing and driving change in this organization, it was impossible to drive the changes in the overall organization without addressing this department, and its manager would be impossible. At the same time, this manager basically told me I ruined an organization she loved. Given the situation, I am not sure how I could have handled the situation any better. However, that is still a line I take with me into every situation to ensure that I am working to handle situations not just with change in mind but with empathy and psychological safety. But there is no doubt that change is hard. There will always be consequences of change that are hard for individuals to handle.

The future of leadership is about always asking, always learning, and never settling for the status quo.

It's hard not to take this kind of opinion negatively but I also have to remain objective. This organization had spent two years in the red (drastically). The organization she loved could not continue without it dying. That's the hard part. My empathetic and objective mentality has always left me sensitive to both sides but able to do what needed to be done. I have always tried my best to lead with empathy, but this is likely an area we can always improve.

FUTURE OUTLOOK ON CURIOSITY AND LEADERSHIP

Curiosity will play an even more vital role in leadership. In an increasingly complex world, leaders must be adaptable and always open to learning. Some of the most transformative moments in my career came when I didn't have the answer but asked, "What am I not seeing?" That willingness to ask and listen opened doors to perspectives and ideas I never would have considered otherwise.

The leaders of tomorrow will be those who embed resilience, adaptability, and a spirit of inquiry into every level of their organization. They'll foster networks of collaborative, curious people who are ready to meet complex challenges with agility. This shift will require leaders to build systems where curiosity and exploration are woven into the very DNA of their organizations.

The future of leadership is about always asking, always learning, and never settling for the status quo—being curious. It's a journey I'm still on—one that has taught me that curiosity isn't about having all the answers. It's about having the courage to keep asking the questions that matter most.

So, embrace curiosity, celebrate the unexpected, and lead with an openness that paves the way for a future of innovation, growth, and change.

Acknowledgments

First and foremost, I have to thank three very special people. My wife and son had to suffer through countless nights of my research, writing, and editing to get this book to fruition. I know and understand that having an entrepreneur as a husband and father is not always the easiest. I thank you both for your tolerance and patience. I would also like to thank my mom for always believing in me. This book is just as much for her as it is for me.

Lastly, there are so many individuals who have been a part of my personal and professional growth. I have worked with many bosses, coaches, and colleagues who have inspired me and pushed me to greater heights. I thank each and every one of you.

About the Author

Jon Bassford, JD, MBA, CAE, is an expert in curiosity-driven leadership. Not your typical operations professional, Jon has applied his curiosity to launch, manage, and improve operations for organizations ranging from venture-backed startups to global nonprofits with far-reaching impact. Known for his relatable and engaging teaching style, Jon is a sought-after speaker invited by top companies and conferences to develop scalable systems and inspire innovative thinking in change-ready organizations. Learn more at jonbassford.com.

If you are interested in seeing how Jon's consulting firm can help you get curious about your organization to drive innovation, growth, and change, learn more at www.think-lateral.com.

Endnotes

[1] "Abraham H. Maslow Quotes," Goodreads, accessed December 18, 2024, https://www.goodreads.com/author/quotes/4570807.Abraham_H_Maslow.

[2] Heraclitus, *Fragments*, trans. and ed. Brooks Haxton (New York: Penguin Classics, 2001), 28.

[3] Sharma, Robin. *The 5 AM Club: Own Your Morning. Elevate Your Life*. HarperCollins, 2018.

[4] Annabel Acton, "10 Einstein Quotes to Fire Up Your Creativity," *Inc.*, August 2, 2016, https://www.inc.com/annabel-acton/10-einstein-quotes-to-fire-up-your-creativity.html.

[5] Michael J. Kramer, "This Doubled Jeff Bezos' Productivity in the First Month of Amazon," *CNBC*, January 7, 2020, https://www.cnbc.com/2020/01/07/this-doubled-jeff-bezos-productivity-in-the-first-month-of-amazon.html.

[6] "Carol Dweck: A Summary of Growth and Fixed Mindsets," FS blog, fs.blog, accessed December 13, 2024, https://fs.blog/carol-dweck-mindset/.

[7] Attributed to Thomas Edison. This quote is widely cited but its exact origin is unverified. For example, see "Thomas Edison Quotes," *The Edison Papers*, Rutgers University, accessed January 3, 2025, https://edison.rutgers.edu/quotes.htm.

[8] Attributed to Winston Churchill. The origin of this quote is uncertain. For further discussion, see Richard M. Langworth, *Churchill by Himself: The Definitive Collection of Quotations* (New York: PublicAffairs, 2008), 576

[9] Attributed to Confucius. The exact source of this quote is unclear and likely apocryphal.

[10] Henry Ford, *My Life and Work* (1922; repr., New York: Doubleday, Page & Company, 1926), 107.

[11] Wayne Dyer, *The Power of Intention: Learning to Co-Create Your World Your Way* (Carlsbad, CA: Hay House, 2004), 60.

[12] "About Blue Origin," *Blue Origin*, accessed January 3, 2025, https://www.blueorigin.com/about-blue.

¹³U.S. Small Business Administration, "Frequently Asked Questions About Small Business," last modified July 23, 2024, https://advocacy.sba.gov/2024/07/23/frequently-asked-questions-about-small-business-2024.

¹⁴ "Timeline: 50 Years of Economic Change and Manufacturing Progress," *Assembly Magazine*, accessed December 18, 2024, https://www.assemblymag.com/articles/85640-timeline-50-years-of-economic-change-and-manufacturing-progress.

¹⁵*Ted Lasso*, season 1, episode 8, "The Diamond Dogs," directed by Declan Lowney, written by Joe Kelly, Brendan Hunt, and Bill Wrubel, aired August 28, 2020, on Apple TV+.

¹⁶World Economic Forum, "Future Readiness: Here's Why Smaller Businesses' Success Matters," *World Economic Forum*, December 2022, https://www.weforum.org/stories/2022/12/future-readiness-here-s-why-smaller-businesses-success-matters/.

¹⁷Winston Churchill, *Churchill by Himself: The Life and Opinions of Winston S. Churchill* (New York: Hachette Books, 2008), 182.

Made in the USA
Columbia, SC
12 July 2025